GROWING
GOOD

INDIANA UNIVERSITY PRESS

GROWING GOOD

A Beginner's Guide to Cultivating Caring Communities

Edited by Bill Hemminger

This book is a publication of

Indiana University Press
Office of Scholarly Publishing
Herman B Wells Library 350
1320 East 10th Street
Bloomington, Indiana 47405 USA

iupress.org

Manufactured in the United States of America

First printing 2021

Library of Congress Cataloging-in-Publication Data

Names: Hemminger, William J., editor.
Title: Growing good : a beginner's guide to cultivating
    caring communities / edited by Bill Hemminger.
Description: Bloomington, Indiana : Indiana University Press, [2021]
Identifiers: LCCN 2021004073 (print) | LCCN 2021004074 (ebook) |
    ISBN 9780253057631 (paperback) | ISBN 9780253057648 (ebook)
Subjects: LCSH: Community life—Illinois—Evansville. |
    Helping behavior—Illinois—Evansville.
Classification: LCC HM761 .G76 2021 (print) |
    LCC HM761 (ebook) | DDC 307.09773/92—dc23
LC record available at https://lccn.loc.gov/2021004073
LC ebook record available at https://lccn.loc.gov/2021004074

CONTENTS

NOTE FROM THE EDITOR

BECAUSE OF THE PANDEMIC, 2020 was a harrowing year for all of us. Events of that year made some of the services described in this volume assume even greater importance while hampering other efforts. The food pantry I now manage, for instance, has lacked many of its regular clientele, mostly because the building that houses the pantry has been closed. We do distribute food nonetheless. At the same time, it has been a challenge for the nearby shelter for women and children to keep up with increased demand throughout the period.

The pandemic also postponed the publication of this book, whose message may be as important today as ever.

Bill Hemminger

GROWING
GOOD

INTRODUCTION

*"Where Do We Come From? What Are
We? Where Are We Going?"*

THE TITLE OF THIS INTRODUCTORY essay is taken from
the famous 1897 painting by Paul Gauguin. It is an enigmatic
work: human and animal figures inhabit a lush tropical land-
scape; the various sizes and groupings of the figures—some
seated, some picking (forbidden?) fruit, several seated near a
sleeping infant, one much older figure crouching alone, a stolid
idol with upstretched arms—together suggest a symbology
that even today remains undeciphered. Yet Gauguin considered this work his masterpiece and scratched the title words

"Where Do We Come From? What Are We? Where Are We Going?"
Paul Gauguin, 1897–1898, Museum of Fine Arts, Boston.
Peter Barritt / Alamy Stock Photo.

onto the upper left-hand corner of the sackcloth canvas. Those words express yearnings that all people share and for which human society might provide plausible answers. And these questions may today be raised again with increased concern for the well-being of others and of our planet.

There has been a wholesale attack on common decency in the United States in recent years. A newly empowered and strident nationalism has sought out and targeted minorities to demonize, denounce, and banish—immigrants, neighbors, Muslims. A vocal, intolerant, and reactionary Christian religious conservatism has publicly vilified other faiths and even other more moderate Christian voices. Environmental regulations and the offices that enforce those regulations have been gutted, and years of environmental protections have come under threat from the very forces empowered to protect that environment. These power-wielding politicos—and their regressive actions—would surely answer Gauguin's questions differently. Theirs would truly be a "new world order," one that is extravagantly selfish, intolerant, xenophobic, and venal.

The United States has not always looked like this. As French traveler Alexis de Tocqueville noted already in the early nineteenth century, there has long been a thriving spirit of voluntarism in this nation. Certainly, part of the impetus of such caring action has been a recognition that not all people gain equally (or at all, sometimes) from general economic well-being, political representation, or the benefits of a democratic society. Sometimes, that impetus is fueled by religious belief and practice: observing Christian tenets has led believers to establish and develop hospitals and care centers, among other altruistic efforts. Often, that impetus stems from no religious injunction at all. We live together in society—now made ever smaller with easy access to social media—and empathetic people are witness to what others lack or need and can work to redress the inequity. In fact, the focus of this volume is precisely these people and how, in these uncivil times, they work to care for the people and the world around them.

This is also a story about *community*, that overused and often-maligned word. For our purposes, community is the social network that usually extends beyond family members and connects individuals to their neighbors, to their towns or cities, and to the land on which those cities are built. For those of us who have spent our adult lives in places where we have no family members, we assert our place in community and our concern for the well-being of that community in acts of common friendship and, often, active altruism. These days, so few caring voices can be heard above the vitriol of Twitter accounts and political invective. *Growing Good: A Beginner's Guide to Cultivating Caring Communities* is a record of some of those other voices, a small chorus of social and environmental justice practitioners from the American Midwest.

· · · · ·

Chapter 1 of *Growing Good: A Beginner's Guide to Cultivating Caring Communities* describes the work of Gleaners Food Bank in Indianapolis, Indiana. The author, John Elliott, was shocked to learn about the large number of people with food insecurity—15 percent of the population—in a prosperous farming and manufacturing state and then determined to work to fight hunger—as head of a large food bank.

Chapter 2, "A Refuge in the City," describes the work of Catholic Charities, particularly their Migration and Refugee Services, which provides succor and care for immigrants in Louisville, Kentucky. The author, Shelley Dewig, has worked as an outreach coordinator and knows firsthand the difficulties—and the triumphs—that recent immigrants have experienced.

Chapter 3 is also set in Louisville, where the Passionist Earth & Spirit Center serves as a site for "healing the alienated and abusive relationship between human beings and the planet." In his essay, Kyle Kramer describes the important, causal connection between environmental action and spiritual growth.

Chapter 4 details the coming-to-activism of a young woman in Evansville, Indiana. Having grown up in the polluted Ohio River Valley, dotted with numerous coal-burning power plants, Wendy Bredhold decided to organize others and fight the "super-polluters." In the process, she has become a powerful community activist.

Chapter 5, written and illustrated by Cris G. Hochwender, a faculty member at the University of Evansville, and one of his students, Anna Jean Stratman, tells the story of the creation, maintenance, and flourishing of a native plant garden on the university campus. Not only does the garden provide a natural balm for the campus, but it also serves as template for those who recognize the importance of appropriate local plants in an endangered ecosystem.

In chapter 6, "A Community of Gardeners," I chronicle the life of a community garden and the people who come together to tend it. Attached to the narrative is a series of poems, all inspired by gardens or garden work.

In chapter 7, Jes Pope provides the history of a shelter for battered women and their children. The House of Bread and Peace was established in the early 1980s. Clients' needs quickly outgrew the capacity of the old wooden house to accommodate them, and the House of Bread and Peace moved in 2002 to a new and more commodious location, still in Evansville, Indiana. It bears its original name and continues to minister to women and children.

Also located in Evansville is Patchwork Central, an intentional community established in 1977. Its current directors are John and Amy Rich; Amy is the author of chapter 8, "Creating Community." Patchwork Central and its long list of dedicated volunteers have for more than forty years provided an array of free programs—many for children and focused on the arts—for the benefit of city residents.

What follows is an album of photographs of Calvin Kimbrough, who has spent a life living in underserved urban neighborhoods and composing pictures of his homeless neighbors. His title for chapter 9 is simple and expressive enough: "Friends and Neighbors."

In chapter 10, three volunteer coordinators with CASA—court-appointed special advocates—describe their work training and assisting volunteers who work with kids taken from their families and who are as a result caught in the court system. Often living in foster care or in youth treatment facilities, these kids gain a voice in court through their CASA and gain a say in their self-determination.

Chapter 11, the work of Kamela Jordan, takes the form of a recommended-reading list. "Books to Open Young Minds" includes lists and descriptions of books organized on a number of timely and underrepresented subjects—Africa, the Middle East, gender and sexuality, disability, and poverty, among others. As the author notes, books can "plant the seeds of understanding, and as understanding grows, fear and hate and condemnation wither away."

The final section, chapter 12, of *Growing Good: A Beginner's Guide to Cultivating Caring Communities* is entitled "The Sweet Spot of Climate Action." The author, Jim Poyser, disgusted with government inaction on climate change, quit his job and started a nonprofit, Earth Charter Indiana, whose goal is to empower young people to work to mitigate the effects of climate change. The opening paragraph to the Earth Charter's preamble is included in this chapter.

Growing Good: A Beginner's Guide to Cultivating Caring Communities is a book for any time: it catalogs efforts of ordinary people to care for their neighbors and their home places. The theme of the book is all the more important today, given the national miasma generated by mean-spirited political cant and counterproductive political action.

To Gauguin's question "Where do we come from?" the answer is historical: we are a nation of immigrants who, for the most part, have welcomed others and other viewpoints to this country. My four grandparents arrived on US shores in the early years of the last century from Eastern Europe, lured by the hope of work and a better life for their families. They were not disappointed. What we are is a group of people who define our community—our place in the world—as part of a social and a physical environment, both of which we acknowledge that we must care for. The view forward, in response to where we are going, is at the moment frightening. Yet many of us are working to better, not impugn, others' lives; many of us are working to preserve, not pillage, our environment; and many of us are working to ensure that it is ordinary people, not a plutocracy, that truly define what we as a nation value.

1

WHY BOTH FEED THE LINE AND REDUCE THE LINE?

John Elliott

AS WE REFLECT WITH APPROPRIATE pride and a sense of accomplishment on the economic success of our Hoosier State, I find myself questioning how those same indicators might also lead to a sense of shame and discouragement if viewed from a different perspective—that of our neighbors struggling with poverty, including the 1 million out of 6.63 million, or 15 percent, of Hoosiers who are food insecure every day. The state of Indiana leads the nation in manufacturing per capita, it was named the most effectively run state government in the nation, and our unemployment rate is the envy of our Midwest neighbors. We debate whether to spend our significant fiscal surplus while our bankrupt neighbor Illinois pays less than 60 percent of its bills. When achieving success, however, it is worth pausing to reflect on who has been left out of that success. I awake each day pondering a series of questions that begin with *why*. In this essay, I'll share some of those *why* questions with you, hopeful that you will react by joining me

CONFRONTING FOOD INSECURITY IN THE UNITED STATES

Gleaners Food Bank is one of more than two hundred Feeding America food banks in the United States. These agencies collect, store, and distribute food to more than sixty thousand food pantries throughout the nation, providing enough food for 4.3 billion meals each year. In 2019 alone, more than thirty-seven million people struggled with hunger; that number includes many children and elderly citizens. Visit the Feeding America website—feedingamerica.org—to find out more about food insecurity in the United States, the history of Feeding America, and how you might help.

in striving toward realistic but daunting and sustainable solutions.

I came to my Gleaners Food Bank leadership role from the board of directors, following more than a decade in a federal government economic and trade policy-making role and residency in other countries, a brief stint in higher education, and nearly twenty years at major corporations. In my public affairs role for the Kroger Company (deservedly labeled by *Forbes* and the *Chronicle of Philanthropy* as the most generous company in America at the time), I oversaw all aspects of community engagement for a multistate operating division. That included more than $11 million annually in support of dozens of hunger-relief organizations, primarily in Indiana and Illinois, clearly the top priority within that division's $15 million annual budget and consistent with Kroger's national community engagement activities.

Combining decades of career and volunteer experience, I've seen both strategic big-picture and neighborhood-centric grassroots realities around the world. Although I came to Gleaners with a business-oriented, data-centric, and policy-level bias toward how I make decisions, as well as a lifetime of fiscally conservative politics, I care very deeply about my hungry neighbors. I am perhaps a demonstration that solutions to social challenges like hunger and poverty can be compassionate, faith based, and yet fiscally sound. If we set aside outdated political and economic assumptions, accept shared responsibility, and focus on people-centric aspirational outcomes, we can identify viable, sustainable solutions. Why can't the best hunger-relief solutions also be the most economically viable and fairest to the people we strive to help over time? They can—when we all come together to construct and refine the best solutions.

As a unified, singularly focused community, we must share a sense of urgency regarding the convergence of hunger and health but also accept the complexity of additional interconnected issues related to hunger. It is hard work and even overwhelming to be poor, especially when the community's attention and resources seem to leap from one politicized priority to the next in isolation. It falls to us, then, not to jump from issue to issue but to remain singularly focused on simultaneous, shared multifactor solutions—accompanied by a disciplined process of sequencing and prioritization.

Hunger is connected to educational success, mental health, chronic health issues, the level of adult productivity on the job, and workplace cultures and norms that need to change. Hunger impacts the overall public good of our community and our shared quality of life. If we focus on health indicators as one example, 34 percent of our food-insecure neighbors have diabetes (versus the national average of 9.4 percent), 58 percent have heart disease, 79 percent purchase the cheapest food items regardless of their awareness of associated health concerns, and the food insecure have 44 percent higher health care costs than the national average.[1] Food insecurity is more predictive than income for the ten most prevalent chronic diseases, including hypertension, coronary heart disease, hepatitis, stroke, cancer, chronic obstructive pulmonary disease, and kidney disease. Hunger brings a higher risk of childhood anemia and hospitalization.[2] There is no better investment you can make than in the health and nutrition of children. I believe there is a connection between Indiana's forty-second-of-fifty-states ranking for quality of public health and the inadequate resources we devote to hunger relief—although certainly there are many other determinants of a state's success or failure.[3] Food insecurity limits children's performance in school in the short term, but more importantly, it limits their physical, emotional, and cognitive growth—with implications over a lifetime of societal cost to others and missed opportunities for the children. This is not the right way to invest in our future generations.

The most effective cure for hunger is a paycheck that supports the entire family for the entire month. So why don't we directly connect and incentivize workforce opportunities and hunger-relief efforts for those with the capacity to work? Can we admit that unemployment rates mask the impact of underemployment on households and the viability of their monthly incomes? Hunger and chronic disease can result in disability, leading to reduced labor force participation, so why don't we make the right short-term investments for long-term economic gain? Why does the state budget in Ohio provide its statewide food bank association more than $20 million per year in resources while Indiana provides $300,000? Is that demonstrative of prioritization? Are Hoosiers pleased to rank thirty-first in the United States for food insecurity?[4] Is that really the best Hoosiers strive to offer each other?

Before pondering further questions, I'd like to share a bit of background information on those we serve: nearly half are children or senior citizens; one in five is a veteran or active-duty military; 64 percent of households report at least one unemployed adult—not 100 percent, as a common stereotype indicates; 70 percent are living at or under the poverty level; 53 percent are in deep poverty with an annual income less than $10,000; 29 percent of households include grandparents raising their grandchildren; 81 percent choose between food and transportation; 78 percent choose between paying for food and medical care; 77 percent choose between paying for food and utilities; and 65 percent choose between paying for food and housing.[5] If we recognize the compelling convergence of hunger and health challenges for families in need, why do we accept stunningly poor levels of obesity, diabetes, and heart disease overall in Indiana—and a dramatically higher incidence for those in poverty?

Ultimately, I hope that the two hundred regional food banks and more than sixty thousand local agencies that comprise the Feeding America national network will go from the largest charity in the United States to irrelevance. I want my job to be no longer necessary. That would be a just social and economic outcome. But it is not happening—and it won't until we change both the dialogue and the way we build, pursue, and evaluate the success of solutions. As we create communities of practice, mobilize outside expertise and technology, and set aside parochial tendencies to genuinely pool resources and define multiyear scaling of solutions, there is a role for every one of you to play and every talent you bring.

Why is one in seven Hoosiers food insecure? At Gleaners, our mission now focuses not only on feeding the line of those who are hungry but also on reducing the line through unprecedented collaboration and communication with other community organizations. We are very mindful of the complexity of interconnected issues related to hunger. Hunger is a long-term challenge that will never be eliminated, but it can be effectively addressed. Gleaners distributed twenty-eight million meals in 2018 and will see a significant increase in our volume in 2019—but there still is a meal gap in every county. A 15 percent increase in meals distributed from 2017 to 2018 means we met 39 percent of the meal gap—and we did not meet 61 percent. Across Indiana, our neighbors miss 170 million meals a year—six million meals in Marion County alone.[6]

In May 2017, Gleaners became one of Feeding America's eight regional produce processing centers, operating a cooperative that will support thirty-nine regional food banks in seven Midwest states. Most important to me, we will have access to dozens of healthy, nutritious produce items direct from the farm—replacing a history of anxiously waiting for old onions and old potatoes to arrive at our back door. Why don't the hungry neighbors we are privileged to serve deserve the same quality and variety of food my family and I have access to? Why shouldn't the amazing farm families and agribusinesses of Indiana feed their hungry neighbors as well as they feed rural Chinese and Central African villagers? Indiana has an impressive long-term record of food exports and our retail food network effectively leverages our geographic location and position as a leading US transportation hub, so why shouldn't food-insecure Hoosiers enjoy raspberries from California, tangerines from Florida, apples from Washington, and melons from Indiana? In 2016, Indiana exported $4.6 billion in agricultural products. The market value of Indiana's top nine agricultural products totaled $6.48 billion in 2017.[7] Surely we could be as proud of feeding hungry neighbors with Indiana pork, duck, and soybeans as we are of our exporting prowess. In 2016, Gleaners did not receive a single pound of fresh produce directly from a farm. In 2018, we received and distributed more than ten million pounds. We need to increase that to at least fifty million pounds. Please tell your federal and state elected officials, as well as Hoosier farmers and agribusiness decision-makers, that they must join with food banks to convert US food waste into food for hungry Hoosiers. Tell them with appropriate urgency.

Why is the world's only remaining military superpower, and the leading economy in the world, incapable of feeding all its people a healthy, nutritious variety of food? We should be far more concerned than we are with wasting up to 40 percent of this nation's food production while our neighbors go hungry. We can feed every American. We simply choose not to. Farmers plow crops under for short-term economic or food retail quality considerations rather than appropriate societal considerations. Feeding America, including Gleaners and 199 peer food banks, distributed 4.2 billion pounds of food to the hungry in 2017, and yet forty-one million Americans still do not have sufficient food to sustain themselves. Are we truly a superpower if more than 12 percent of US households are food insecure?[8]

A choice between national security and food security is not necessary in leveraging dollars taken from taxpayers. The US can afford both, but you need to raise your voice in advocacy —making that realistic expectation clear to elected officials at the federal and state levels. At the same time, Gleaners and every other hunger-relief charity needs your resources. Ideally, we need cash to buy the most needed, most nutritious food from food companies who sell to us at very deep discounts. We no longer seek loose food donations that come with high supply chain costs, no ability for nutrition and menu planning to benefit clients, and no transparency in the event of food safety recalls. Please consider going to www.gleaners.org /donate to support my very hardworking team of staff and volunteers, https://feedingindianashungry.org/ for partner food banks elsewhere in Indiana, or https://www.feedingamerica .org/ways-to-give to find a food bank in need outside Indiana. We all desperately need your time, talent, and resources.

Why do myriad poverty-related charities compete for community resources and the attention of our elected leadership instead of collaborating on shared solutions? A very distracting reality hovering over us every day is the 82 percent of all hunger-relief meals in Indiana provided by four federal programs: Supplemental Nutrition Assistance Program (SNAP—previously known as food stamps), at 58 percent; Women, Infants & Children (WIC), at 3 percent; the Emergency Food Assistance Program (TEFAP), at 2 percent; and school lunch programs, at 19 percent.[9] By comparison, despite being the largest hunger-relief charity in Indiana, Gleaners' share of meals provided to the hungry in our twenty-one-county service area is 8 percent.

Nationally in FY2018:

- ■ TEFAP commodity purchases—a program of bulk US Department of Agriculture (USDA) commodity purchases to stabilize specific US food-industry sectors, then distributed by the Feeding America network—totaled $288 million (this does not include a supplemental, temporary series of USDA purchases intended to offset the impact of tariff disputes with major US trading partners in 2018 and 2019);

- Partial reimbursement for some of the TEFAP storage and distribution costs borne by food banks totaled $64.4 million;

- SNAP distributions through state agencies totaled $74 billion;

- WIC distributions through state agencies totaled $6.175 billion;

- Commodity Supplemental Food Program (CSFP) programs focused on helping specific populations through approved agencies, such as meals for senior citizens by Gleaners and the Central Indiana Council on Aging (CICOA), totaled $238.1 million; and

- School-based breakfast, lunch, and after-school nutrition programs totaled $24.2 billion.

Any substantive change to these USDA programs would have a devastating impact on our work, as the partial shutdown of the federal government in late 2018 and early 2019 and the lack of an approved funding appropriation for the USDA's social programs clearly proved. In the most recent federal fiscal year, 12 percent of Indiana households received SNAP benefits, with a high rate of 22 percent in Fayette County and a low rate of 4 percent in Hamilton County. Of particular concern, 21 percent of Indiana households with children under eighteen relied on SNAP benefits.[10]

The most frightening scenario facing the social welfare of our state is the possibility that our federal government proceeds with oft-threatened dramatic cuts to the SNAP and other food-program funding with no time to implement alternatives that do not even exist today. Gleaners is not capable of suddenly increasing from 8 percent to 25.4 percent of meals for hungry Hoosiers in our service area. Mobilizing our entire safety net of nonprofit and state agency resources would not close the gap. We must protect federal hunger-relief programs as the nonprofit sector continues to build capacity to feed and concurrently reduce the lines of hungry neighbors. Food banks like Gleaners and other community-based hunger-relief organizations are not passively waiting to react to federal policy but are actively working with federal and state agencies to drive entrepreneurial, innovative ideas that will make these federal programs successful initially, albeit replaceable later. That includes USDA Farm to School Grants, the Farmers' Market Nutrition Program, the Summer EBT Program, and the Summer Food Service Program. I struggle to imagine a more unjust scenario than thousands of local hunger agencies closing their doors with one million hungry Hoosier neighbors still outside. We must advocate effectively for appropriate and affordable client-centric outcomes. There are also roles to play for individuals, corporate citizens, institutions of higher learning and research, local foundations, and others in designing viable replacements or supplements to the federal programs. Please consider lending your subject-matter expertise and that of the organizations you are connected to in support of these efforts.

In the meantime, Gleaners occupies the second-largest food bank building in the country, at three hundred thousand square feet—a source of consternation, not a sense of accomplishment. If you combine our cash budget of more than $10 million and the food value of $56.2 million, our $66.2 million annual budget makes us one of the largest social service charities in Indiana. I'll be very honest—I wish we needed to be very small. I wish we didn't need the help of ten other regional food banks and two thousand local agencies to still fall short of feeding every hungry Hoosier. From 2010 to 2014, Gleaners moved to a much larger building, doubled the number of meals we distribute, more than doubled our fleet, quadrupled the amount of fresh produce distributed, grew our staff by more than 50 percent, and nearly bankrupted the organization to briefly close the meal gap in our twenty-one-county service area. But then the federal government changed the SNAP funding formula twice in 2015, and all that phenomenal progress was erased. Indiana suddenly had a two-hundred-million-meal-per-year gap again, since reduced to 170 million meals. Until we design a system that solves hunger concurrently with interconnected poverty challenges—a system not dependent on the political and fiscal whims of Washington—sustainability and viability will remain elusive.

Why do traditional social solutions imply that the individual factors of poverty can be resolved one at a time in isolation? Families face a daunting interconnected mix of poverty challenges simultaneously, not separately. Even the federal poverty line is no longer a clear indicator. More than 39 percent of families living above the poverty line are food insecure. Other factors that influence food insecurity include local cost of living, household structure, social capital, and the mix of public benefits received.[11] Hunger is connected to educational success and quality of life, to mental health and chronic health issues, and to workforce productivity and economic success. Ultimately, it impacts our shared quality of life.

Why does our community dialogue continue to focus on budget allotments within one fiscal year when the most appropriate measure is cost avoidance over one or more lifetimes and maximizing opportunities while minimizing opportunity costs for every citizen? The food we eat is critical to our health, especially obesity, diabetes, and heart disease. That's why hunger is responsible for at least $77.5 billion per year in additional medical costs in this country, or $1,800 per food-insecure household.[12] Unless nonprofit, for-profit, and public sector organizations assess these poverty challenges together, agree how to measure success consistently, collaboratively develop solutions, and implement those solutions simultaneously amid unprecedented communication, we will never solve any of the individual factors of poverty. Investing in hunger relief today will save every sector of our community and our economy many, many times more over time. If the opportunity cost of not feeding children and investing in their greatest potential lifetime of contributions is considered, our short-term fiscal caution ensures an overwhelmingly negative opportunity cost. Thankfully, there are solid indications of evolving process and dialogue. Indiana health systems are becoming very innovative in linking social determinants of health to their resource investment priorities and patient outcomes.

Frankly, I hope I've intruded in your thoughts and perhaps even caused you sufficient discomfort that you will share my sense of urgency and will feel empowered to go forth, joining us as we both feed the line of hungry Hoosiers and reduce the line by helping to solve all their interconnected challenges simultaneously. I am hopeful, on behalf of our neighbors in need, that you will accept our shared responsibility and impose that sense of shared responsibility on our elected officials. I hope also that you feel compelled to reach out not only to Gleaners but to any of the intensely hardworking hunger-relief and poverty organizations in our state to dedicate yourself to solving the interconnected challenges of poverty, hunger, and health. Why should we strive to solve only hunger? Why not all interconnected factors of poverty? Why just Gleaners working alone? Why not you? Please . . . .

Gleaner's Food Bank of Indiana: https://www.gleaners.org/

JOHN ELLIOTT leads the largest hunger-relief charity in Indiana, distributing twenty-five million meals per year to 320,000 hungry Hoosiers in twenty-one counties. He has considerable international experience, serving ten years as a diplomat with the US Department of State in Washington, Burma, Taiwan, and Thailand, focusing on regional economic and trade issues involving China, Japan, ESCAP, and the United Nations. A graduate of Hanover College with a BA in business, John also earned his MBA from Butler University and completed studies in Mandarin Chinese and Asian studies from the US Foreign Service Institute in Washington.

Notes

1. Feeding America, *Solving Hunger Today and Ending Hunger Tomorrow*, 2018, https://www.feedingamerica.org/sites/default/files/2018-11/2018%20Feeding%20America%20Annual%20Report_0.pdf.

2. Feeding America, *Solving Hunger Today*.

3. McKinsey & Company, *Best States 2017: Ranking Performance throughout All 50 States* (US News & World Report, 2017).

4. McKinsey & Company, *Best States 2017*.

5. Feeding America, *Map the Meal Gap 2017*, 2017, https://www.feedingamerica.org/sites/default/files/research/map-the-meal-gap/2015/2015-mapthemealgap-one-pager.pdf.

6. Feeding America, *Map the Meal Gap 2017*.

7. Indiana Department of Chamber Research Department, USDA, *2019 State Agriculture Overview*, 2019, https://www.nass.usda.gov/Quick_Stats/Ag_Overview/stateOverview.php?state=INDIANA.

8. Feeding America, *Solving Hunger Today*.

9. Indy Hunger Network, *Revised Hunger Study*, 2017, https://www.indyhunger.org/studies-reports/.

10. Indiana Department of Chamber Research Department, USDA, *2019 State Agriculture Overview*.

11. Alisha Coleman-Jensen et al., *Household Food Security in the United States in 2016*, Economic Research Report Number 237, Economic Research Service, USDA, September 2017.

12. Feeding America, *Solving Hunger Today*.

2

A REFUGE IN THE CITY

Shelley Dewig

> "Migrants and refugees do not only represent a problem to be solved,
> but are brothers and sisters to be welcomed, respected and loved."
>
> —*Pope Francis, World Day of Migrants and Refugees, 2014*

IT WAS RAINING THE DAY Abdullah (not his real name) shared his story with me. That day, I was at the local library, at a mentoring activity I had helped organize for a local refugee resettlement agency. I remember wondering how he was going to get home in such inclement weather. As we packed up to leave, it began to pour and suddenly turned very cold. I asked him if he had a ride home, and he assured me he would walk. After some arguing, he finally relented to let me take him. I drove the five blocks to his house, and what should have lasted one minute ended up taking four hours as he began to tell his harrowing story about how he fled from his former life in northern Iraq. He was a Christian living in a Muslim-majority country, and he and his family had been targeted by numerous Muslim extremist groups for many months. He and his family had received death threats at home, work, and school, so he said he had to make the hard decision to leave. He took a taxi to the airport and flew to Turkey, where he lived alone for about a year. There, he applied for refugee status as he struggled to find work. Later, he arrived in Louisville, Kentucky, where he knew no one. His family was still back in Iraq, and he was worried that something bad would happen to them. As he told his story, he would go back and forth through different time periods of his life and his emotions, and he would take long pauses while he tried to continue. I could tell that he was reliving his journey all over again for the first time since arriving to Louisville. After he finished, he seemed drained but also lighter, as if a weight had been lifted from him. He apologized for keeping me so long and said, "I haven't told anyone my story yet, so I just needed to get it out."

That day changed my life forever. I had been working with refugees for several months, but I had never heard anyone's story in such detail. I realized that everyone I had met in those months had similar stories, and yet here they were in the US, acting completely "normal." I was dumbfounded at the realization that humans could suffer such trauma and still find jobs, laugh at jokes, and make the decision to get out of bed every day. As I've gone through my career working with refugees and immigrants, I am always astonished at what they manage to accomplish after living through their ordeals.

I currently work as the parish engagement and outreach coordinator at Catholic Charities of Louisville, Kentucky. My job is to connect the faith and secular communities to the work we are doing at Catholic Charities, especially within our largest department, Migration and Refugee Services (MRS). I help recruit volunteers and get them to work, solicit material and financial donations, plan special events such as our World Refugee Day, organize refugee camp simulations, and speak about issues pertaining to refugees and immigrants. It's an exciting job to which I have felt called in part because of Abdullah's story. I am incredibly grateful for this work.

MRS is a department of Catholic Charities whose mission is to provide refugees support and services needed to ensure early self-sufficiency (ideally by the third month after arrival). MRS was formed in 1975 and is the oldest refugee resettlement agency in Kentucky. We have resettled almost thirty thousand refugees from thirty countries. Currently, we are resettling people from Bhutan, Myanmar, Cuba, Haiti, Somalia, the Democratic Republic of the Congo, Rwanda, Burundi, Eritrea, Ivory Coast, Syria, Iraq, Iran, Pakistan, Afghanistan, and South Sudan.

Before refugees arrive, we furnish an apartment or house and purchase food for the family. We pick up the refugees at the airport and transport them to their new home. Then we provide orientations, apply for public benefits, enroll all children in the public school system, teach adults English, transport clients to medical appointments, and, from time to time, help adjust immigration status. Finding a job is the most important factor in early self-sufficiency, so our employment team works to orient clients to workplace culture, apply for jobs for clients, take them to interviews, and conduct follow-ups. All these programs rely on talented staff members and community volunteers so that our refugee clients can find the path to independence as soon as possible.

We have the capacity to serve upwards of 1,200 clients a year. The number of refugees we resettle depends on a presidential determination, which sets the national number of refugees allowed into the country. During the 2016 fiscal year, the Obama administration set the cap at 110,000, but because of the travel and refugee program bans over the last several months, the US resettled only 53,000. Catholic Charities in Louisville was prepared to resettle 700 refugees, but we ended up serving 480. In this fiscal year, which began October 1, President Trump limited the number of refugees allowed into the US to 45,000, the lowest number since the Refugee Act of 1980 formalized the resettlement program. Because of the shrinking refugee population, our national agency, the United States Conference of Catholic Bishops, had to lower our projected number for the upcoming year to 330. As one can imagine, our staff has struggled with such a tumultuous and uncertain year. With drastic cuts in funding, we went from a staff of forty-six to twenty-six in a matter of months. For a while, as other resettlement agencies around the country were closing, we weren't sure what the future held for us.

Though we have been discouraged by negative public rhetoric and funding cuts to the refugee program, MRS has been overwhelmed by the outpouring of support we have received from people in neighboring communities. Organizations, churches, and individuals have come out to stand with us at rallies, volunteer at special events, and donate. To their government representatives, they have written letters of support for refugees. They have risked their reputations and sometimes livelihoods because of their support. This certainly is a time when you must speak out in order to be on the right side of history.

As Pope Francis stated during the 2014 World Day of Migrants and Refugees, refugees are our brothers and sisters; we must welcome them. Here is a short list of ways you might become involved:

1. Mentor a family and help them learn English while aiding them in getting to know their new home.
2. Be a daycare assistant for refugee babies and toddlers while their parents attend English classes.
3. Set up apartments and grocery shop for incoming refugee families to create a welcoming space for them.
4. Organize a donation drive for your local resettlement agency (or for us in Louisville if you don't have one!).
5. Advocate by writing letters in support of the resettlement program to your representatives in state and federal governments.
6. Attend legislator meetings with us, represent your field, and tell representatives why allowing refugees to resettle in our community is important.

In whatever time you have, you can do something. Anything big or small is a step toward justice.

Catholic Charities has always been deeply engaged in social justice issues, whether those issues concern refugees, undocumented immigrants, women, children, or minorities. Our leadership has supported legislation and encourages all citizens to welcome strangers and care for those who are oppressed. We have partnered with many faith-based and secular groups to increase our broader support.

Abdullah eventually got work at a ceramics factory and then at UPS. In addition, he has worked as an interpreter for us here at Catholic Charities. Since his arrival, he has married and now has a beautiful little daughter. Abdullah was fortunate enough to arrive here, and he was welcomed, respected, and loved by supporters like you. We will continue to need strong voices in the fight against oppression, and we would love for you to join us.

Catholic Charities of Louisville: https://cclou.org/

SHELLEY DEWIG is the parish engagement and community outreach coordinator at Catholic Charities of Louisville, where she has worked for more than three years. Prior to that, she worked as the Cuban/Haitian case manager and AmeriCorps VISTA volunteer coordinator at Kentucky Refugee Ministries. In addition to working with refugees, she has taught English in Morocco and at universities in the United States. Shelley has been fortunate to work in international nonprofit organizations for ten years. She has a BA in French and international studies and an MA in international development.

3

MADE FOR BELONGING

Spiritual Practice and the Pleasures of Bridge Building

Kyle Kramer

I. Interconnection and the Great Work of Our Time

I work in Louisville, Kentucky, where I run the Passionist Earth & Spirit Center, a nonprofit interfaith spirituality center founded and supported by a Catholic religious order. Shortly after the 2016 elections revealed such deep divisions in our country, we invited our program participants to an impromptu gathering so that, together, we could process our reactions in a safe, supportive space. There was a stunned, shell-shocked quality to that gathering as people struggled to understand what the election meant for the future of our country. I remember one of the attendees, an accomplished cardiac surgeon from Pakistan, wondering out loud if he still knew his adopted country and whether he was still welcome here.

The Earth & Spirit Center's mission is to help bring about what ecological writer Thomas Berry called the "Great Work" of our time: healing the alienated and abusive relationship between human beings and the planet that sustains us. For Berry, the shift in cultural consciousness that the Great Work requires is a paradigm shift more profound than any in modern human history. Put simply, we need to understand—in our minds, hearts, souls, and bodies—that we are fundamentally and inextricably linked to each other and to all of creation. We flourish together, or we perish together, as individuals, as communities, and as a single planet-scale ecological system. This truth of interconnection and interdependence must be lived out not only in the choices we make as individuals but also in the cultural, governmental, educational, and economic structures that undergird our common life.

The ideas I have just written are not new. Though they have been emphasized by recent discoveries in modern science, you can find similar sentiments in many great philosophers and religious thinkers, both East and West, as well as the world-view of many indigenous peoples, stretching back thousands of years. The ideas may not be new, but they never caught on very broadly.

II. The Paradox of Our Historical Moment

For two reasons, we're at an interesting moment in history—both human history and the deep-time geological history of our planet. First, the human race has become so numerous and so technologically advanced that we have become a geologic force unto ourselves, with the power to make drastic changes to the basic operating parameters of the natural world. Given that we now have it in our power to bring ourselves and countless other species to extinction, it has never been more critical to start cultivating a deep understanding of our interlinked fates.

The great paradox of our historical moment, however, is that just at the time when it's most critical for us to overcome our differences and work together in support of our common good, we feel more divided than ever. Our partisan politics are paralyzed, our social groups are balkanized, and our civic life and public institutions seem to be weaker and more withered with every passing day. Many of us are some combination of angry, terrified, disempowered, and hopeless—especially as we see the appalling, strident intolerance of newly emboldened fringe groups.

III. Spiritual Practice: To Change the World out There, Attend to the World in Here

I am not especially optimistic by nature, but in the past several months, two experiences have given me some measure of hope that we poor human beings might begin to live more fully out of the better angels of our nature. The postelection gathering I described was of diverse spiritual seekers holding many different religious (and nonreligious) beliefs, who nonetheless shared a fundamental conviction: the world out there will not be changed until the world in here changes. Yes, we need to get right to work transforming all the unjust systems and structures that foster intolerance and that make it so hard to be good. But unless we do some deep spiritual and psychological work, we won't make much headway in changing the externals—and in fact, we will ultimately just keep re-creating them. The truth of interconnection can really only sink in when our own egos and unhelpful personality structures aren't completely running the show. And in the aftermath of the 2016 election, I saw more and more people committing themselves to that interior work.

A BEGINNER'S GUIDE TO MEDITATION

1. Find a time and place in your day where you won't
    be disturbed by digital devices or other people. You
    can start with just five minutes; eventually you may
    want to work up to twenty or thirty minutes, once
    or twice a day, as you have time and desire. Use a
    timer of some sort (with a gentle tone) so you don't
    have to watch the clock.

2. The right posture is key. Although it's certainly
    possible to meditate lying down, sleep is always a
    temptation. You can eventually invest in meditation
    cushions (known as *zafus* and *zabutons*), but
    you'll probably find it easiest to start with a simple
    straight-backed chair. You want to be relaxed but
    not slouching, alert but not tense, with a straight
    back, head level, and arms resting comfortably on
    your lap.

3. Close your eyes or look down with soft focus and
    half-closed eyelids.

4. Take note of how your body feels, firmly grounded
    and stable in its position. Without trying to control
    your breathing, take notice of your breath moving
    gently in and out of your body.

5. You will almost certainly be bombarded by a
    barrage of thoughts, feelings, and sensations.
    Don't fight any of them, and don't expect your
    mind to clear. Simply notice each one, with
    kindness and curiosity rather than judgment. Then
    let it go; a helpful tool is to imagine watching
    your thoughts as if they are boats floating by on

a stream. The thought will likely return very soon; don't be frustrated when it does. The "practice" of meditation isn't in not having thoughts and feelings but in simply noticing them when they arise and letting them go so you don't get hijacked by them and follow them down a ruminative rabbit hole.

6. Don't feel the need to focus continuously on your breath, but the breath is a good way to restore your attention when your mind has wandered away with your thoughts.

7. Again, don't be hard on yourself if you don't feel especially peaceful or have a busy "monkey mind." Most of us do. Remember, the goal is not to get rid of thoughts but to become less attached to them: to observe them, noting whether they are pleasant, unpleasant, or neutral, and then let them go. This is especially true for itches, aches, and pains. Don't torture yourself, of course, but be willing to sit with some discomfort.

8. When your timer goes off, allow yourself three slow breaths to come back to attention (if your mind has been wandering), and then gently end your practice with compassion for yourself and all beings.

9. The fruits of meditation are generally most obvious not in the practice itself but in the rest of your life. Notice to what extent you're able to be present and kind in your life circumstances and a little less reactive, perhaps having more mental focus and clarity. You can experience such benefits from meditation in as little as a few weeks' practice.

At the Earth & Spirit Center, for example, we have taught thousands and thousands of people the basic practices of mindfulness meditation. Beyond all the hype it enjoys these days, mindfulness—like other contemplative practices—offers some helpful tools for examining our personal and collective shadow and for cultivating a consciousness of connection rather than alienation. It also provides much more clarity, nonreactivity, and emotional resilience in the midst of trying circumstances. Our current cultural situation of alienation and intolerance makes it clear that such contemplative practices are not simply hobbies for those with spiritual inclinations and leisure time but crucial responses that support the health of our common life and our planet. And I see more and more people committing to incorporating them into their lives, even as they are also committing to taking on more active roles in their neighborhoods, local governments, environmental challenges, and ailing social institutions.

IV. The Pleasures of Bridge Building

Work, work, work. The inner work and outer work I described earlier are good and necessary, but as I read back over what I've written, I realize that there may be a roll-up-your-sleeves, grit-your-teeth, eat-your-spinach quality to it, which is far from what I intend. Although hard work and discipline are part and parcel of cultivating a healthy inner life and a healthy civic life, the most fundamental fuel for real social change is the deep pleasure and satisfaction of building bridges, as we explore both our inner reality through contemplative practice and our outer reality through our efforts for social change.

Lest this sound too heady and theoretical, let me share a second experience that underlines my point. Louisville is an interesting place: on the one hand, it still has deep divisions of race and class, such as the famous "Ninth Street Divide," which persist from the city's earliest days; on the other hand, Louisville is a sanctuary city, welcoming refugees from all over the world and providing support services to help them acclimate. I became more directly aware of the plight of refugees this year, when the Earth & Spirit Center partnered with Catholic Charities and another local organization to establish community gardens for refugees (mainly from the East African nations of Burundi and Congo) on the twenty-seven-acre property of our spirituality center.

Almost all of these men and women were farmers and gardeners in their home countries, and they now live in housing situations where they have no access to land. In addition to the trauma they experienced in their native countries and in the refugee camps (where some of them spent almost two decades), they now face the disorienting task of adjusting to a country, language, culture, and economic system that are entirely new to them. Having been an organic farmer and gardener all my adult life and having lived through the excruciating process of leaving a farm I loved, I am grateful to help provide them this opportunity to reconnect with the soil. Now nearing the end of their first growing season, the refugee gardeners are feeding about 150 family members from their meticulously tended plots.

One afternoon, as I was leaving work, I discovered that a friend had left me a beautiful loaf of homemade wheat bread. On my way to my car with it, I saw that two of the refugee growers were working in the gardens, so I brought the bread over to them. We managed to overcome the near-total language barrier with pantomime and some laughter, as they took a break from their work and we broke the loaf together. I have never tasted better bread or had more pleasure in sharing. I'm looking forward to our end-of-season potluck harvest festival to celebrate their successes and connect them with other community members who are interested in the project or have supported their work. The growers are planning skits, African drumming demonstrations, and tours of their gardens.

They are proud of what they have accomplished, and I am thrilled to see how profoundly healing it has been for them to work together "out in the nature" growing their native crops, which they cannot otherwise find or afford in their new homeland. They already have big plans for next year: additional acreage, a greenhouse, more beehives, and, in a burst of extreme optimism for our urban property, cows and chickens and goats. I haven't yet had the heart to gainsay even the most farfetched of their hopes; I imagine that even to dream about such possibilities means a great deal to them in light of the experiences they have had.

In the face of the divisiveness and intolerance that is sweeping across global and national stages right now, the Earth & Spirit Center made a conscious effort to reach out and build a bridge to a group of people who live on the margins of our society and, to some extent, have been unfairly made into scapegoats for our national woes. We made this decision out of principle, but what we have ended up with is pleasure: the joy of connecting to fellow human beings, across continents and cultures, through our common love of the land and of good food. It has been work, but it has been the good and deeply satisfying work of love.

V. Made for Belonging

I believe that deep in our biological, spiritual, and cultural DNA, we are made for belonging—in our human communities and in our whole-Earth community. Unfortunately, we seem to be in a national moment of intolerance that makes it easy to forget the fundamental truth of our interdependence. Fortunately, however, we are not without resources: the inner spiritual practices that are never more than one breath away from any of us, as well as the outer satisfactions of building bridges to others we do not know and to a future for which we hope.

Passionist Earth & Spirit Center: https://www.earthand spiritcenter.org/

KYLE KRAMER is the executive director of the nonprofit Passionist Earth & Spirit Center in Louisville, Kentucky, which offers interfaith educational programming in meditation, ecology, and compassion. Kyle and his family spent fifteen years as organic farmers and homesteaders in Spencer County, Indiana. Kyle serves as a Catholic climate ambassador for the Catholic Climate Covenant, is a former columnist and essayist for *America* magazine and a current columnist for Franciscan Media's *St. Anthony Messenger* magazine, and is the author of *A Time to Plant: Life Lessons in Work, Prayer, and Dirt* (Ave Maria Press, 2010).

4

STANDING UP TO THE
SUPER POLLUTERS

Wendy Bredhold

MY CLIMATE ACTIVIST JOURNEY BEGAN just over a decade ago, when I read in an Associated Press report in the local newspaper that Evansville, Indiana, the city where I live, has some of the nation's poorest air quality.

When I read that AP report in 2006, there was little public acknowledgment of the Evansville area's air-quality issues. I was shocked and outraged to learn that here in this midsized city in Indiana, surrounded by farmland, we are breathing some of the worst air in the country.

I showed up at a Meet Your Legislators forum organized by the League of Women Voters to voice my concerns, and I met three other women—Jean, Carly, and Kim—who were there for the same reason. They were all mothers—I wasn't yet—without a lot of time and didn't want to organize formally, so we created an informal web-based group we called Air Aware, with a mission of simply informing the public about our heavy

HOW TO GET ORGANIZED

1. Find your tribe. It's so easy now to find people who share your interests through various online forums. Who cares about what you care about?

2. Find the activists who are already doing the work. They are always looking for volunteers and can plug you into activities where you can make the greatest difference. There is so much opportunity to take leadership.

3. Know your community and your representatives. Do you have a neighborhood association? Who is your representative on the city or county council? Are there town halls or forums where you can meet your local and state representatives? When do the staffs of your members of Congress have local office hours? Meet them, talk to them, and tell them what you care about.

4. Don't give up. Working in these groups can be difficult. People will have strong opinions and personalities, and there will likely be conflict— within groups and between groups. Take that as an opportunity to work on your leadership and interpersonal skills and hang in there.

5. I repeat: don't give up. You won't change the world overnight. But you can make a difference. I don't know many things to be true, but I believe absolutely in these words from Margaret Mead: "Never doubt that a small group of thoughtful, committed, citizens can change the world. Indeed, it is the only thing that ever has."

burden of pollution and holding those in power accountable for it in any way we could.

None of us were organizers, but I had some experience in activism within the antiwar movement, and as a former reporter at a local newspaper who was then working in media relations, I knew how to get messages into the public eye. We also had a whole new set of online tools available to us, as it was the early days of online communities and social media.

We wrote letters to the editor, wrote comments on online newspaper articles, emailed public officials and talked to them at public forums, and spread our message through the media. Carly came up with a particularly creative publicity stunt when she put a bag of polluted air up for auction on eBay. A local television station gave her coverage, interviewing her on a playground with her children, holding the bag of air.

We also were able to learn a lot from a longtime local environmentalist who had a watchdog group called Valley Watch. He told us the names and offices of the people who were supposed to be informing the public when air quality was particularly bad. We began to hound the City of Evansville Environmental Protection Agency office and Vanderburgh County Ozone Officer with questions about local polluters, and when they did issue air-quality alerts, we raised the alarm and asked media outlets why they weren't distributing the information.

My daughter was born five years after I read that AP story, during record heat and a week of air-quality alerts. When she was one year old, I was accepted into Al Gore's Climate Reality training and, inspired by the former vice president's message, decided that air quality and climate would be my life's focus.

Soon after, I emailed the director of Moms Clean Air Force, a children's health organization with a focus on air quality and climate, and I offered to start a chapter in Indiana. I had discovered the organization—a project of the Environmental Defense Fund—through social media, and as I was a new mom, their mission really appealed to me. I received an enthusiastic reply, was invited to become a blogger on their website, and eventually was offered a part-time position as an organizer in Indiana while I continued to work full-time at a university. With MCAF, I worked to generate support for stronger environmental rules at the federal level—regulations targeting mercury, smog, soot, and carbon emissions—that would protect our families where we live. I even got to travel to Washington, DC, and meet with EPA administrator Gina McCarthy to ask her for stronger protections from coal plant pollution. I brought a picture of my daughter to show McCarthy on a day that Evansville had the worst air quality in the country.

In 2015, I learned that the Sierra Club was looking to hire a campaign representative for their Beyond Coal Campaign in Southwest Indiana. I've rarely wanted anything more than I wanted that job and the opportunity to work on the issues I was most passionate about full time, and by that time, I had collected a range of abilities and knowledge that seemed perfect for it.

For the last few years, I've worked for the Sierra Club: Beyond Coal, first as a campaign representative for the Lower Ohio River Valley and now as senior campaign representative for Indiana and Kentucky. Along with allied groups, our teams of staff and volunteers are engaging directly with electric utilities, the commissions that regulate them, city leaders, state legislators, governors' offices, and federal officials to make the case for a clean energy transition in Southwest Indiana and across the state and country that will protect our health, create jobs, save money, and avert a climate crisis. It's tough work, but I wouldn't want to be doing anything else.

The Sierra Club: Beyond Coal: https://content.sierraclub .org/coal/

Before **WENDY (KNIPE) BREDHOLD** became the senior campaign representative for the Sierra Club's Beyond Coal campaign in Indiana and Kentucky, she was the Indiana organizer and blogger for Moms Clean Air Force, worked in media relations and taught communications at the University of Southern Indiana, and wrote for various newspapers and magazines in Indiana and Kentucky. She is a 2012 Climate Leader in Al Gore's Climate Reality Corps and served on the Evansville (Indiana) City Council. She lives in Evansville with her daughter, Beatrice Rose, and cats, Pearl and Pinky.

5

MAKING YOUR GARDEN NATIVE AND NATURAL

Cris G. Hochwender and Anna Jean Stratman

DEDICATING EVEN A SMALL PORTION of your garden or yard to growing plants that are native to your region can have a beneficial influence on your community. Native plants feed native insects and provide food resources to other animals. They also compete with nonnative weeds and reduce the need for pesticides, and some native plants add nitrogen to the soil, reducing the need for fertilizers. Unfortunately, habitat destruction has led to the loss of wetlands, prairies, and forests, resulting in reduced numbers of native plant species. Although parks and conservation areas help maintain native populations, the land dedicated to these sites does not provide enough area to sustain biodiversity. As one would expect, the loss of floral diversity has caused a reduction in the number of herbivores (animals that eat plants) and pollinators (bees, butterflies, moths, and birds that fertilize flowers). Pollinators search flowers for food—nectar and pollen; as they feed, they move pollen from one plant to another, helping plants reproduce. The reduction

MAKING YOUR GARDEN NATIVE AGAIN

The Native Plant Finder is a website hosted by the National Wildlife Federation where anyone can enter in their zip code and learn what plants and butterflies are native to their region. Visit the site at https://www.nwf.org/NativePlantFinder/. When deciding to use native plants, consider the following suggestions:

1. Native plants are often pollinator friendly; native plants also provide food for herbivores (like butterfly and moth larvae). Learn more about native plants from local organizations like the Indiana Native Plant Society (INPAS: https://indiananativeplants.org/).

2. Plant a diversity of native plants; greater floral variety provides food for a greater diversity of pollinators, so choose a range of flower colors and shapes for your garden.

3. Similarly, choose a mixture of plants that flower in the spring, summer, and fall; seasonal variation in flowering provides food resources for pollinators across the growing season.

4. Reduce or eliminate your insecticide use. Many insecticides that kill pests will also kill beneficial insects.

5. Support land conservation in your community. Organizations like the Sycamore Land Trust (https://sycamorelandtrust.org/) protect valuable habitat in Indiana.

The University of Evansville's native plant garden in Koch courtyard

in habitat that supports these herbivores and pollinators has had a negative effect on natural communities. Growing native plants in urban areas provides a space for native plants and helps support these animals.

The University of Evansville's (UE) native plant garden represents one effort to restore native plants. The native plant garden was proposed to UE's president as a feature to enhance environmental science and biology experiences. The garden was started in the spring of 2011, replacing seventy by eighty feet of lawn on campus. In just three years, the first plants filled the area so completely that the area became a mature garden. The UE's native plant

Black-eyed Susan

garden now provides a venue where more than one hundred species of native flowers, grasses, shrubs, and trees can be viewed.

Although many plant families contribute to the high diversity in this garden, the most diverse family—both in this garden and in North America —is the sunflower family. Dozens of species in this family, including the cup plant, black-eyed Susans, and coneflowers, are easily identified by the ray and/or disc flowers that compose each multiple-flowered head. Herbs in the mint family, such as bee balm, are also found in the garden. These herbs are distinguished by their square stems and fragrant odors when the leaves are crushed. One other important plant family in the native plant garden is the pea family (Fabaceae). Species in the pea family convert inaccessible

Top to bottom: Beebalm; Monarch caterpillar feeding on common milkweed; Monarch butterfly on thin-leaved milkweed

nitrogen for plant growth, which enhances the soil, promoting greater species diversity. Plants in the pea family have one of three distinctive flower types, including the easily identified pealike flowers and their fruit pods.

The wide variety of plants available in the native plant garden provide protection and even food for a number of local herbivores. Some plants provide food for dozens of herbivore species, and a few tree species can provide food to more than three hundred different herbivores. Plants with unique toxic chemicals deter most herbivores from feeding on them, but other herbivores, including monarchs and swallowtails, use odor cues from unique chemicals to search out their host plants.

While we often recognize butterflies as generalist pollinators, they are feeding machines when they are caterpillars, often incorporating plant toxins for defense against their predators. For example, monarch caterpillars feed only on milkweed species. In addition, milkweed flowers come in a variety of colors and forms, providing "food" for the gardener's eyes. Milkweeds produce cardiac glycosides, a toxin that prevents most herbivores from feeding on milkweed plants (and most also produce a sticky, milky latex—giving the milkweed its name). Monarchs incorporate the cardiac glycosides as a defense against their predators. Without milkweeds, the monarch butterfly would go extinct.

With its orange-and-black wings, the monarch butterfly is the most easily recognized insect in North America. Because it is easily identified, monarchs serve as an emblem or state insect for seven states, one Canadian province, and one Mexican state. Government agencies partner with conservation organizations in a variety of programs to monitor and alleviate human impacts on the monarchs. Moreover, nonprofit organizations engage citizens across North America to support its annual migration.

In part, the investment in monarch protection stems from the inspirational migration that takes monarchs from their winter home in Mexico, northward through the United States, into Canada, and back to Mexico the following fall. Five to seven generations are required for monarchs along their journey, with monarch females laying eggs on milkweeds to start each new generation. To complete this migration successfully, land for milkweed conservation must be preserved in the Midwest, Canada, and Mexico. These conservation efforts are increasingly important, as monarch butterflies face a number of threats (for example, application of herbicides that kill milkweeds) to their success across North America.

While monarch butterflies may inspire people to conserve and grow native plants,

Top to bottom: Swamp milkweed; Butterfly milkweed; Bumblebee on Joe-Pye-weed

conservation of native bees is important because bees are exceptional pollinators. UE's native plant garden provides resources for many pollinator species (including butterflies, beetles, flies, and birds), but native bees are in critical need because of habitat loss and insecticide use. Moreover, bees are wonderfully diverse; more than four hundred species of bees occur in Indiana alone. A variety of bee species can be found at UE's native plant garden, including many bumblebees.

While butterflies, bees, and other native animals have benefitted from the native plant garden at UE, many local gardeners in Evansville have also committed to growing native plants in their gardens. This larger community has also started seed exchanges that share native seeds to enhance

Top to bottom: Bumblebee pollinating a purple passionflower; Bumblebee on purple coneflower; Skipper butterfly pollinating a purple passionflower

each other's native plant diversity. In the spring of 2019, a group of UE students even created a community outreach class to promote native plant awareness in the Evansville community. These students have grown and given away one thousand milkweeds in an attempt to bring awareness to declining monarch populations, to educate the public about the importance of using native plants in their backyard, and to engage people in thinking about the ecological value of such refuges for herbivores, pollinators, and the rest of the native community. Consider joining these efforts to improve your community.

DR. CRIS G. HOCHWENDER earned his bachelor's in biology at Cornell College, completed his PhD in biology at the University of Missouri–St. Louis, and has carried out research in the area of evolutionary ecology for more than twenty-five years. His research has explored plant defense against herbivores, plant tolerance to damage, local adaptation of plants, and structuring forces of arthropod herbivore communities. More recently, as a faculty member in the biology department at the University of Evansville, he has addressed questions that center on restoration ecology, including questions in tropical forest restoration, wetland restoration project in Indiana, and the use of native plants to recruit their native insects.

ANNA JEAN STRATMAN graduated as an environmental administration and biology major at the University of Evansville. For the last two years, she has performed research studying monarch oviposition preferences and has developed her research into a community engagement project. After graduation in 2019, she began pursuing her master's degree in environmental conservation management at the University of Wisconsin–Madison.

6

A COMMUNITY OF GARDENERS

Bill Hemminger

MY FAMILY AND I MOVED to Evansville, Indiana, in 1990, where I had accepted a position at the University of Evansville in the Department of English with additional teaching responsibilities in the Department of Foreign Languages. In rural southeast Ohio, we left a newly built home, located in the countryside not far from Athens. We also left a community of wonderful friends—family, really—with whom we had lived for more than a decade as good neighbors and who had nurtured my wife and me as well as our two young daughters. The new home—built by a good friend who was also a talented contractor—replaced an early 1800s log cabin, our first home there; that much-loved ancient-wood structure burned on March 6, 1989, while my wife, my daughter Johanna, and I were in Madagascar, where I was teaching at a university under the aegis of the Fulbright program. The loss of that cabin was not unlike the loss of a close family member, so emotionally attached were we to the dirt-displaying logs and the company

HOW TO CREATE A NEIGHBORHOOD GARDEN

1. Who are the gardeners? How will you contact them? What are they willing to commit to? What would they like to see in the garden? In our case, I make a contact list of people interested in garden work (colleagues, neighbors, students, friends) and then send out messages explaining when I'll be working in the garden and on what tasks. Newcomers are always welcome. Garden work, especially in the humidity and heat of southern Indiana summers, is *much* more tolerable when done as a group, so it's always gratifying to see ten or more people converging on our green space. Not only does the work finish faster, but gardeners get to know one another as they work as well.

2. Decide what sort of garden you want.

   A. Is open land available nearby? A vacant city lot? Somebody's backyard? Can the space be tilled up easily? Our garden space is a gift from the University of Evansville, and I make a pilgrimage each year to the president of the institution to make sure that the garden space is still ours and not the site of yet another sports field.

   B. What about raised beds (helpful in the event that the ground is hardpan or full of trash)? They can be built cheaply of recycled materials, filled with good soil (which can be made), and set at a height convenient for most gardeners. The soil in each bed must be regularly improved with compost (which can be made in your kitchen or backyard).

C. Then there are container gardens. Almost anything can be a container—from an old shoe to an unwanted pot or trash can (provided there is drainage, which can be created by puncturing the base of the boot or can). An old boot might be a fine home for a basil or thyme plant; a wooden box might support tomatoes or peppers. Containers can fit anywhere, which is a benefit, though they dry out quickly and require regular monitoring.

D. How is the produce to be distributed? In our case, gardeners determine what and how much they want of the garden produce. What is left (always *lots*) we take to sell at a farmers' market on campus, where we sell produce very cheaply, partly as a return on the free use of university land but also as an inducement to get people to buy produce they might not know how to cook or eat (what money we make goes into the budget for the following growing season). We've made a number of converts to beets, for instance (red, pink, golden), as well as Swiss chard, and have surprised even seasoned cooks with new flavors of basil. Then, when the market has ended, what produce remains goes to a local food bank. Nothing is wasted.

3. Get together to have fun—enjoying the products of your labor and the fruits of your kitchen. Gardening work is good work: it feeds both body and spirit.

of forest critters that came to visit us in our domicile; the first poem, "Outdoor Life," suggests some of this attachment. Just after the fire, we returned from Africa to reconstruct our lives and build a new home when I got news of a better job in a small city in the boot of Indiana.

So we left our rural life in the gentle hills of southeast Ohio, among people we knew well and loved and whom we had vowed never to leave—to move to a small city (more of a large small town) close to the institution where I worked. At first, we occupied a small apartment near campus where a closet was the only available space for the crib of our six-month-old daughter, Mollie. Soon enough, though, we found and bought a sturdy brick house, also close to campus, and began our new lives as quasi-city dwellers.

But the livin' was not all that easy. I missed the relative cabin quiet, occasionally interrupted by turkey calls or the bleating of my sheep, and I longed for the proximity of meandering streams and steamy "hollers," where I could stumble-walk among fire pinks or sycamore saplings or wander the open ridge tops, edged by secret outgrowths of bright-orange bittersweet and home to private glimpses of sunsets or the gathering of white-tailed deer at dusk. Instead, we inhabit a forest of strip malls close to a river whose ebb and flow can be read in the rings of rubbish that attach to its banks. And we traded the close communion of a few consanguineous neighbors for the democratic but somewhat disorderly assortment of city dwellers. The poem "Modern Motions" describes this exchange.

In Evansville, I was drawn to the land but in a way so that I could be productive too. In those early years, I was part of an intentional community, one whose focus was, among other things, to help people in the surrounding neighborhood blocks in the city core value and care for their homes and their city. The community owned an empty half lot behind the main building, and though that lot was regularly disfigured by trash trucks that cut the alley corner too soon and left deep ruts in the dirt, ruts that filled with broken glass and indeterminate city trash, the lot represented a challenge—to try to make a cast-off, forgotten part of town both productive and beautiful.

So the first garden program was born. I hauled over a large tractor tire, flopped it on the alley corner to discourage future shortcuts, filled it with dirt, and planted a prickly rosebush. Then I set about removing years of ground-up trash, replacing ruts with loam and planting four blackberry canes, a natural hedge against incursions, the gift of a friend. The garden plot moved annually to the west after that: each season, I'd dig ten or more feet of the shrinking lot and commit it to intentional planting. Buried bricks from forgotten, collapsed buildings would climb to the surface of the soil as we dug; we put them in piles and later used them to create and pave a meditation garden whose floor bricks are arranged in an elegant herringbone pattern. Then we added fruit trees in honor of friends and some berry bushes in memory of others. Thereafter, for a number of years, I would leave my university office early a couple of days a week, change my clothes, and rush across town in my little car to work with young people in various children's programs as they tilled soil, planted seeds, weeded, harvested, perspired, played. It was my garden community.

One of those kids is the Zach of the eponymous poem; he was a fan of the thickly grown blackberries. And the other kids delighted in the rows of sunflowers, *Helianthus annuus*, that grew tall in our garden and became feeding stations for summertime goldfinches as well as the subject for my poem. Also always a hit with the program participants was the late-fall digging of sweet potatoes, celebrated in the poem of the same name, swollen sugary suns that outlast the waning of summer rains and hide just below the surface of the soil. Gardens can

WRITING POETRY IN RESPONSE TO GARDEN WORK

Well, poetry is charged language—that is, language carefully considered and arranged in particular ways for a purpose. We are regularly bombarded by cheap, pandering blather—on the radio, on TV, in various media—and poetry (both writing and reading) offers an occasion for us to seriously consider the words we use and how to use those words judiciously to depict an emotional reaction to the land and to people on it.

What comes first—the subject or the form? No easy answers here; most poems arise from considerably less than conscious thought or intention. It is most important simply to begin, perhaps a word or two on a piece of paper (or in cyberspace). Most poems undergo major transformations as they develop; in other words, where the poem begins is not necessarily where it may find safe harbor finally, which is, of course, fine. If yours is a formal work, why have you chosen that form? Does it suggest anything about the subject? Can the form you use add a dimension of meaning to what the poem is trying to describe or say?

Don't be afraid to let the poem rest for a while, even a long while. Sometimes what you thought you were aiming at is lost in a later reading, though something may have been gained in understanding. Words can touch deep reservoirs of feeling in us; writing poetry is thus a recipe for reaching to less than conscious parts of ourselves and trying to retrieve a fair statement of what we are able to find.

Sometimes a little research is helpful. I enjoyed
reading about sunflowers, their cultivation and growth,
the history of their partnering with human society, and
the implications of the name in various languages.
Then I made a number of choices to create my poem
"*Helianthus annuus.*"

be the site of important learning, horticultural and not, and of
great beauty, albeit seasonal. In the bigger picture, we hoped
that the kids might see these city lots differently, might envi-
sion their lives differently, especially since they had had a hand
in creating the edible beauty. Of course, the suburban zeal for
weedless lawns of unnatural grass or rigidly cropped shrubs—
the impetus for the poem "Green Gulag"—is but an extension
of this manhandling of earth and seed. Yet I'd like to think that
gardeners work *with* natural forces to shape and sustain their
gardens and that gardens might transform our cities and urban living spaces and remind us that we—as stewards—live
on and with the land.

That garden program flourished for a number of years. Then,
sometime after returning from a second Fulbright, this time to
Cameroon, I asked our university president if I might transform a large field on campus—stretching along the highway
that bisects the city—into a campus garden. After a couple of
seasons of rocky starts (quite literal since the field was really
the smoothed-over remains of a row of houses that had been
demolished, with insulation, bricks, cement blocks, and other
bits barely buried), our garden program took shape. The current site is about 75 by 250 feet, and a line of fruit and nut

Spring crops and rototiller

trees separates our produce from the noisy, polluting express-
way. To passersby, I figure that the garden may serve as an
emblem of health and vitality in a region that typically values
neither. To us garden workers, it is the site of our labor and the
source of our togetherness.

It has always been a goal of mine to involve as many people
as possible in garden work, which can have spiritual as well as
physical qualities to it. For four years now, I have employed a
student worker throughout the growing season, and this collaboration with college students has in each case been wonderful (reciprocally, I'd like to think). A couple of constituencies at
the university offered funding for a paid position, and I came
up with a syllabus of sorts. It has been instructive for me to get
to know and work with college students in the garden context;

we have shared far more than weeding zeal and excitement at picking the first tomatoes or pulling the first Chioggia beets. In addition, a number of faculty colleagues have helped with garden work. Just this year, a biology professor very generously made available her greenhouse in which we started tomatoes, peppers, eggplant, and basil. Then she assigned her horticulture students to work in the garden under my tutelage. At least six other colleagues, all living close to campus, also devoted much time to the garden. Several neighbors also joined the garden group, a couple driving in from the next town; a couple of homeless guys showed up to work from time to time throughout the season. At two different occasions, we benefitted from the labor of student groups (on Freshmen Volunteer Day, curiously now a standard practice on college campuses) and the campus employees who volunteered their time on a campus workday.

Throughout the season, my charge to all participants has been the same: you are welcome to take from the garden in proportion to what you feel you have contributed. Throughout the season there has always been more than enough produce for all of us to return home with plenty of vegetables. With what is left, we have run farmers' markets on campus in June and July. On these occasions, we lug baskets and flats of produce to campus, open up shop inside the student union, and sell great quantities of vegetables for very low prices. In this way, I feel that some people who might be wary of a certain vegetable might, for not much money, buy and try it. We've converted a number of people to partisans of kale or butternut squash or beets, which has been gratifying. The money I collect from these events is put back into the garden—defraying costs of plowing, keeping the tiller gassed up and alive, paying for hose and replacement tools, and purchasing seed and plants in the spring.

Getting the tables ready for the farmers' market

Clover and sunflowers in a frame of pears

Then there is always much produce left. At the time of this writing, the 2017 season is not yet finished, and we have already delivered more than one thousand pounds of fresh beans, potatoes, peppers, tomatoes, summer and winter squash, broccoli, beets, eggplant, and herbs to a local food pantry. And I err in my measurements on the side of modesty. Tended carefully, the land can be so productive. And how wonderful that the work of tending can bring people—of various ages and life experiences—together in the hopes of nourishing ourselves and others as we work with mysterious (and often capricious) natural forces to foster the growing of beauty (see "Seeds of Doubt"). The results of garden work need not differ much from the fruits of writing—both can be salubrious; both can counter cheapening forces of contemporary social life. And in this era of growing xenophobia coupled with an active disrespect for the world that houses us, how important that we create occasions for people to come together to cultivate the land and human relationships.

BILL HEMMINGER taught for twenty-five years in the Departments of English and Foreign Languages at University of Evansville and was chair of the Department of English. An Africanist by training, Bill has published poetry and personal essays in addition to academic works and a collection of reflections on his life and work in Africa, *African Son*. A musician, he has written a number of choral works that have been performed throughout Indiana.

Outdoor Life

The woods moved into
me. That was price
of living there.

Hickories became my standard
for height and hardiness,
sassafras for fragrance, and
isolated white sycamores still
measure the bluest skies.
The shaly hill shadowed
me from west afternoon heat
and taught me small. The
occasional creek murmured:
dying is only temporary.
The hollow burbled with water
long after rains had run out,
and unexpected fire pinks
flanked the feet of elms in
dry weather. I learned that
growing is its only explanation.
Along the west ridge, a row of
pines stood tall against the
winds. Evergreen sentinels
sheltered deer, framed still in
winter viewing. That valley
held me close. Fugitive coons
that carried off my prize Rock
roosters became the masters of
craft. A possum stuck pink
articulated fingers inside the
back window once; I thought

it was a child's hand. A pair of
shy woodpeckers, rapping at
the decaying locust tree, daily
shared their family chatter.

I left that valley, traded
concrete for clayey loam,
chased deer and coons to
parks. Yet neighbor oaks
still tower. In the breach of
buildings, they reach for
sun. I seek their shade.

Modern Motions

We moved to a city: I had to find and dig
in vacant lots that would accept tomatoes,
beets, squash vines growing thick on land
once grabbing at the feet of giant trees and
doused in annual excess from nearby river.
I had to see the single hollyhocks that
thrive along neglected alleys full of easy,
undecaying trash as champions of beauty,
not refugees from failed Edens. I had to
view occasional oaks as emblems of a fallen
forest, grown fuller now for lack of arbor
competition. I had to wonder at the carpet
of spring beauties in the highway median—
an unexpected park for high-speed visitors,
a token of the land's past life. And then I
had to find a place with people. It is not
easy making peace with others, sharing
more than highway lanes or shrinking
supermarket space. We have so many
reasons to hide inside, apart from others'
difference. Now, people mostly make
demands; they do not recognize that what
is best for all can also be good for one. Or
recognize that hollyhocks grow rarer and
statelier because they tower over trash,
that spring beauties beam pink at nearby
asphalt, the humbling limit of their growing.

Zach and the Blackberries

Zach and the blackberries grew
up in the same place, these urban
fields of failing, forgotten houses,
whose chipped and faded
painted walls stop shiny, empty
junk food bags in flight and
keep them pinioned there, the
brilliant birds of dead city nests.

So, too, the blackberries, grown on
ground rescued from asphalt
sprawl, kept clear of wayward
trash trucks, harbor renegade
wrappings from someone else's
feeding. They grow where no
one thought or cared they would.

Neighbors, the two had never
met. I gave the boy a basket;
told him to pick the blackest, fattest
berries; leave the hard red
aggregates on fuzzy stems. Unlike
the walls of homes Zach knew,
these plants were thornless, only the
upward sweep of vine, small windows
between the clumps of healthful fruit.

Black berries crowded the tall plant
walls. They yielded easily to his
fingered tug and fell big into the basket
bowl. That Zach could touch and take

these gifts was grace enough, but
how they tasted!—new and sweet and
subject to his child's touch. Then Zach
could feel the move from earth, to
plant, to hand, and finally to mouth.
For once a cycle other than collapse.
The earth's offering he took within;
it fed his flesh and mind. He now has
roots, though fragile, in the place he's
lived for all his city-child years.

Helianthus annuus

The Italians call it *girasole*; the French, *tournesol*.
The botanist explains that its head, *capitulum*,
is made of many blooms, all of which have *corollae*.
The Russians grew to love the plant and eat the seeds
when Lent forbade the luxury of oil at table.
Somewhere in the canyons of America, the aboriginal
stalks looked up from Havasupai villages to the sun.

What a gift to the growing world this
plant whose great head faces and follows
the sun, as the French and Italians say,
whose radiate head burns with floral
intensity, storing oil in those countless
seeds, each of which can, in moist and
dirty dark, become the plant that grows
taller in two months than we will grow
in years and that has patiently sat for
countless artists and photographers,
who rightly confuse its face for the sun.

Sweet Potato

October, after heat and lack of rain. Soon
evening vapor will collect and congeal
cold on thirsty leaves at night,
then explode in early icy light.
White death in a garden of brown.
To save itself, the sassafras dropped half
its crop of leaves, sclerotic crisps.
Lacking attractive dipping pools, bees
buzz and strafe my sweaty head.

Rampant on the crumbling floor, the sweet potato
vines flow in green and purple waves.
We lug shovels and spades, not worried
we interrupt the purple growing.
We know the swollen orange tubers wait,
gravid there beneath the mantle,
what Mississippi women took as antidote to aging
before science made estrogen a fact of pharmacies.

And though we have gone through all this before,
each heft of the shovel that strikes sweet gold
brings on a gasp and then applause. In thirty minutes
we've destroyed the purple world but don't regret,
since now we eye amazed the growing pile of suns
whose energy is radiant now and stored for later.

Green Gulag

My neighbor thinks that
lawns cry out for edging,
the work of those loud
machines that chuff and
belch. My neighbor trims
forsythia, removing next
year's flowers in his zeal.
The summer flowers he
finds too ragged and whacks
them with a tool. Their heads
drop like chaff. He scrapes
and pulls at the bare spot
in his lawn. The nearby
lively grass conspires to
keep from growing to cover
up the spot. Even passive
grass can be pushed too
far. Late October brings
down red oak and golden
maple leaves; my neighbor
blasts the fallen canopy
with gas-driven windbag,
while later winds will spin
the leaves again to rest
wrapped up in yew and
boxwood for a winter's wait.
My neighbor needs to manage
everything and on his terms.

My neighbor, friendly
fascist, whose kingdom
yields, dumb and green.

Seeds of Doubt

It's May, the soil's fertile, you
know all that; there's lots of
rain, but still the look of that
flat lot, those dry finite tiny
seeds, the head-start weeds
already spreading leaves, their
roots entrenched beneath your
hard-shelled, shriveled eggs—
you can't imagine it, though
you have seen it every year:
from this dead potential comes
the vining trailing abundance
of July, when that seed you
buried doubtfully becomes
a source of leaf. Somehow
despite the sciences of knowing,
the seed has sprouted magic, and
you were witness author to its
work. Each year it has occurred
like this, and every time those
seeds appear so small, so unalive,
so without hope for growth.

Does this propensity for doubt
prepare us to be each time
surprised as if this were the first
coming-into-being? Or is this
doubt itself the seed of holiness,
which dry and lifeless mixes with
the dirty elements of daily living
and makes mysterious an ordinary
moment, makes out of dirt a life?

7

SISTER JOANNA'S HOUSE OF BREAD AND PEACE

Jes Pope

IN THE EARLY 1980S, THE House of Bread and Peace began as the vision of a Benedictine nun who wanted to serve the poor. The House of Bread and Peace originated with a Christmas dinner in 1979. Sister Joanna Trainer said that as the dinner concluded, guests wanted to take all the leftovers. Seeing this hunger shocked her; she decided she had to do something about this. In November 1982, Sister Joanna and her friends started a soup kitchen in Evansville's St. Paul's Episcopal Church. Still running today, that soup kitchen opens on Saturday and operates entirely by donations from a local hospital. It is staffed by dedicated volunteers, who cook and serve each meal.

Seeing the great need of hungry people who came for meals each Saturday, Sister Joanna worried about where they would go at night, especially the women and children. As she got to know these women, Sister Joanna learned that many of them lived on the streets, in unsafe places like cars or "trap houses" (drug houses), or in situations of domestic violence.

So Sister Joanna and her friends decided to start a Catholic Worker house to help some of the most vulnerable women in Evansville.

Started by Dorothy Day and Peter Maurin in New York City in 1933, the Catholic Worker movement created "houses of hospitality" across the globe. Today, there are 240 Catholic Worker communities in the world. The House of Bread and Peace is one of six houses in Indiana. The *Catholic Worker* is also the name of a newspaper still sold for a penny in New York City. Dorothy Day's philosophy was formed by the Gospels, especially Matthew 25:35–36: she sought to feed the hungry, give drink to the thirsty, shelter the homeless, clothe the naked, visit the sick, and visit those in prison. Dorothy Day was Sister Joanna's inspiration; if she could do Jesus's work of showing love and hospitality to the poor, then Sister Joanna could too.

Dorothy Day came up with the concept of a "stranger's room," a room in each home where hospitality could be practiced. Also known as a Christ room, it was kept for any stranger needing shelter. After several years of praying, planning, and searching, Sister Joanna bought the original House of Bread and Peace for $8,500 in August 1984 from Permanent Federal Bank.

Located at 516 Adams Street in downtown Evansville, this bright-yellow two-story home needed a lot of care and attention to make it livable. Many friends and volunteers pitched in to make possible the opening of the doors of the house on an extremely cold winter morning in January 1985. The house was the first shelter of its kind serving women in the Evansville area. Two women who had been living on the street were the first guests Sister Joanna sheltered at her new house.

The house had eight bedrooms and could ideally accommodate seven to nine women and children. But needs increased, and Sister Joanna would sometimes share her home with more than twenty guests at a time. At one time a house dog named Tinker and her puppies lived at the house too. In these early days, the house was closed during the day and open in the evening, since Sister Joanna was still working as a teacher.

Over the ensuing years, the needs of the shelter increased, and Sister Joanna retired after thirty-four years of teaching to devote all her time to the homeless women and children at the house. She strove to provide a loving atmosphere for women to rebuild their lives. She said, "I don't want just anything for the poor. I want the best for them. I want them to know they are loved." She welcomed homeless women just as they came, many carrying only the clothes on their backs. She treated her guests with unconditional love, dignity, and respect.

The warmth and caring are tangible at the House of Bread and Peace even today. The women who come to the House of Bread and Peace come from every upbringing, every financial background, and every race and religion; all share the desire to become independent again. "We do not try to change the women," Sister Joanna used to say. The house has opened its doors to an immigrant mother and her two small boys as they were seeking US citizenship. Not judged by race, religion, illness, or previous failings, women in need are welcomed to the house: women who struggle with drugs and alcohol addiction, women who have been abused, women who are pregnant, women with children, women who are convicted felons, women coming out of prison, women who have lost their jobs, women with physical and mental disabilities, the uneducated, victims of poverty, and young and old. At Sister Joanna's House of Bread and Peace, women enter a real home, not an institution.

The original house on Adams Street could not meet the growing needs in the city. Sister Joanna was troubled by the number of homeless women she turned away daily, some on the phone, some at the front doors. In 1992, the house had just celebrated its ten-year anniversary from the opening of the first soup kitchen, and by that time, the number of guests had doubled. It was time for a larger space, and the fundraising began. There were car washes, barbecues, line dances, quilt raffles, and public luaus—all to raise money. Sister Joanna befriended homebuilder Don Gore and his son, who built a new House of Bread and Peace at 250 East Chandler Avenue just blocks away from the "old" house. Sister Joanna moved to her new home on June 30, 2002.

A number of local companies, banks, donors, and volunteers contributed to the creation of the new house. This beige six-thousand-square-foot home has twelve bedrooms upstairs and a handicapped-accessible bedroom downstairs, office space, storage rooms, four bathrooms, two laundry facilities, a large pantry, five refrigerators, two freezers, two dining rooms, a large open kitchen with two stoves, and a fenced-in backyard with two garden sheds and a playset. In the new structure, Sister Joanna could share her home with up to twenty-six guests at a time.

Dorothy Day has said, "If you put hope where there is no hope, you will find hope; love where there is no love, you will find love; peace where there is no peace, you will find peace." Sister Joanna's passion to help the poor, along with her dedication and persistence, created a place that has become a home to hundreds of women and children over the past thirty-three years. Sister Joanna provided a warm place for desperate and vulnerable people, and she provided an opportunity for them to enjoy life again. In 2004, Sister Joanna left the house in the hands of Sarah Wolf, who had worked in the shelter since she was an intern at a local mental health facility in the 1990s.

Having only three full-time staff, the house has no maintenance or cleaning crew. The staff become the plumbers, the IT team, and crisis intervention. As of this writing, the staff members include Sarah Wolf, executive director; the house manager of sixteen years, Shelley Carter; and former resident and current night manager Patricia Wells. As Sarah Wolf says, "It's not a job, it's part of who we are. It's part of our family." The house is governed by a volunteer board of directors, who donate their time and energies to the management of the house. Volunteers fill in the gaps; many volunteers are former or current residents. The house is always open—twenty-four hours a day, seven days a week.

The only time the house ever closed its doors was in October 2016, when the shelter got bedbugs. It was closed for four days while poisonous gas filled the rooms. Preparing for the extermination was terribly chaotic; all the furniture had to be positioned in the middle of every room, much like a real-life game of Tetris. And food in the refrigerators had to be thrown away. Some meat was saved in specially packaged bags and stowed in the deep freezers. What couldn't be shoved into the back of the minivan had to be thrown or given away, including many toys. Then the house resembled a set from a sci-fi movie, with elongated tubes tunneling throughout the many rooms.

All residents had to figure where they might stay for those four days the shelter had its doors closed. Some stayed with friends, others went camping, and some stayed in their cars. After absorbing the cost of $7,000, the house was reopened, bedbug-free. All that money had been donated. Now, the house follows a strict protocol to prevent another outbreak. Donated items are limited, and each month a local exterminator comes with a bedbug dog from K-9 Detection that sniffs every room of the house. When a new resident moves into the house, the motto now is "What can't go through the dryer can't go upstairs." Those "un-dryable" items are put in totes and locked in the shed until the bedbug dog comes. So far, these practices have worked.

Many people who visit the house for the first time have false preconceived ideas of what a shelter might be like. They have a vision of army cots lined in single row or multiple bunk beds crammed into small concrete rooms. But it's not like that at the House of Bread and Peace. A former resident (who had come to the house directly from prison) has put it this way: "At the house, you are welcomed with open minds, open hearts, and opened arms." A typical room at the house resembles a college dorm room, with two beds, two dressers, and a closet to share with a roommate. Two large family rooms have queen-size beds and bunk beds, and three smaller rooms have playpens or toddler beds for women with babies or pregnant women. While living at the house, resident guests receive all their basic needs: a homey and safe environment, food, clothing, personal items, and love and support. Giving a tour to a family of four just moving into the house, Sarah points out the fully stocked pantry and says, "If you go hungry, it's your own fault."

Most of the donations come from local people. Wal-Mart, Target, and upscale stores like the Fresh Market provide weekly donations of food. Sometimes, the food donations are so great that the House of Bread and Peace can share with neighboring nonprofits, local shelters, Fire Hose House #1 down the street, and neighbors. Outside, there is a "free tree," where neighbors know they can find random usable items—like Halloween costumes, dishwasher detergent, a barbecue grill—for the taking.

During the seasons of Lent and Advent each year, a local Catholic church focuses on giving to the house. In Lent, the church sends more than two large trucks filled with grocery bags to the house. The same church provides Christmas gifts for residents during Advent. "Before coming to the house, Christmas was sad and lonely," said a former resident and current volunteer now living in her own apartment. "I remember being overwhelmed not just by the gifts but by the love and laughter." Each year, the Christmas tree overlooks the gifts—new clothes and boots, housecoats, art sets, racetracks—that spread beneath. In the middle of the tree hang Sister Joanna's most cherished ornaments, two rose-colored turtledoves.

Resident guests are responsible for daily chores and for working on personal goals. The main goal for everyone is to move into safe, affordable, permanent housing. Some women must find jobs and pay off old bills; others will apply for Supplemental Security Income (SSI, a.k.a. "disability") and follow through with medical appointments. All women must continue with their goals for improving their life situations, and everyone completes intake and exit interviews, tracking improvements they have made.

On intake, women are linked with appropriate community resources. Case managers from community agencies come to the house to provide information about programs, resources, and growth opportunities. Some agencies come weekly, providing a familiar face and an occasion to build trust. All these agencies are partners in restoring balance to these women's lives. A former resident notes that "the house provided me the chance to take advantage of many resources and gave me a safe place to lay my head until I could remember how to fly." She is now a college graduate and company manager.

The house operates on a tight budget, serving residents for about sixteen dollars per person, per day. As of 1992, the house is a 501(3) nonprofit. It does not receive funds directly from the Catholic diocese, although churches of many faiths support the shelter.

Before experiencing homelessness, most residents had jobs and raised children. For so many of these women who live on the margins of financial security, though, an abusive relationship or the loss of a job can end their freedom. But balance can return to their lives, and the women can return to independence. A disabled woman with no income applied for SSI and obtained housing. A military veteran with a five-year-old found appropriate housing. A young woman who had lost custody of her son and had come to the house right out of substance-abuse treatment is three years sober now, working full time and juggling the daily duties of raising an eight-year-old. Circumstances can improve, or, as a current resident says, "We are given a second chance and room to grow."

The work of the House of Bread and Peace echoes what Dorothy Day said in 1946: "What we would like to do is change the world . . . By crying out unceasingly for the rights of the workers, of the poor, of the destitute. We can throw our pebble into the pond and be confident that its ever-widening circle will reach around the world."

Sister Joanna's House of Bread and Peace: https://sites .google.com/site/houseofbreadandpeace/

JES POPE is currently a volunteer at Sister Joanna's House of Bread and Peace and a former resident there as well. She graduated from the University of Evansville in 2013 with a bachelor of arts in psychology and creative writing. This is her tenth publication; her other works are included in various journals and magazines.

8

CREATING COMMUNITY

Amy Rich

IN PATCHWORK CENTRAL'S FORTY YEARS, tens of thousands of people have passed through our doors. Whenever Patchwork's doors are open, people come in. They may be young or old; living in poverty or living on comfortable incomes; white, black, Hispanic, Asian, or Native American; men or women; gay or straight; disabled; mentally ill; veterans; or alone or part of large families. It is our goal to treat every one of them with respect, no matter who they are.

Many come in for our Neighborhood Hospitality: for a cup of coffee and a donut, for a place to charge their cell phones, for a loaf of bread and some fresh produce, for some dog or cat food for their pets, to use our phone or fax machine, to rest in our library, to try to figure out where to go for help with their rent or utilities, to take a shower, or simply to have someone to talk to.

Last year, we logged more than nine thousand instances of this kind of hospitality. This number includes 1,150 showers for individuals who, for various reasons, had no other access

HOW MANY SERVICES CAN ONE AGENCY OFFER?

Patchwork Central was founded in a lower-income neighborhood in downtown Evansville, Indiana, in 1977. Since that time, Patchwork's doors have been opened to all, and staff and volunteers have offered innumerable programs. The list of past and present Patchwork programming is long and varied:

- Garden vegetables for neighbors and low-income families
- College and seminary internship programs
- Work to keep a neighborhood school open
- Dental program
- Counseling program
- Protests of nuclear energy and utility rate increases
- Health care services
- Women's advocacy and speaker series
- Summer children's activities
- Transitional housing for women
- Peace and justice speaker series
- After-school children's activities
- Food pantry
- Bakery to employ neighbors and provide healthy food
- Special witness for peace and justice

- Small business training and microloans
- Presence in the neighborhood and neighborhood advocacy
- Relationships with nonprofits improving life in rural Central America
- Men's residency program
- Mennonite voluntary service unit
- Health clinic
- Tutoring within children's activities
- Office and meeting space for many other nonprofits and organizations
- Outdoor art and gardens to be enjoyed by neighbors
- Music activities for children
- Adult creativity classes open to all
- Back-to-school supplies for children
- Dance, bike repair, walking, computers, and small business classes for children
- Clinic space for organizations serving Spanish speakers and people who are HIV positive
- Food co-op to bring healthy food to a food desert
- Gallery space for emerging artists
- Bicycles for adults who need transportation
- Pet food for pets in need
- Health ministry

to shower facilities. We also served up well over one thousand pots of coffee.

I am often in and out of Patchwork's main office when our guests are talking to Dee and Shawn, our office assistants. Dee and Shawn also share stories with me from their experiences in the office. Through these stories, I am very aware that we are living in a broken world full of injustice.

We see good people working so hard to stay ahead of their monthly bills—water, electric, medicine, food, rent, mortgage payments—only to have a setback, such as a temporary layoff, an illness, a significant home repair, or car trouble, arise and drag them down. We see wonderful people who care about others and who share a laugh with us in the main office, but who can't break their addictions. They disappear for a few months, then reappear, telling us they've gotten themselves cleaned up again. We see people who are stressed by their living situations and who are trying to make good decisions, but whose stress clouds their decision-making. We see people who have done terrible, inexcusable things in the past but who are here now asking for help.

My job at Patchwork is rewarding—I feel as though I'm doing something meaningful and worthwhile. I don't lack the resources to live the way I want: simply yet comfortably. As I travel through our city, I am generally greeted with respect. I do not live a life severely limited by injustice or oppression.

I want that for all our guests. I believe that God wants that for them, as well, and that Jesus, in the way that he relates to the poor, the outcasts, and the ostracized, provides us with real-life examples of how to bring them justice.

As I speak with our guests, I imagine what justice might look like in their lives: what would bring about the wholeness and completeness that I believe God would want for them. I imagine jobs for those who are able to work that would pay their living expenses and allow them to stop feeling the stress of being one small problem away from losing everything. I imagine flexible employers able to incorporate unusual souls into their workforce. I imagine alternative opportunities for those unable to work that would provide them with a way to feel they are making meaningful and worthwhile contributions to society. I imagine safe and affordable housing for everyone. I imagine healing for addicts, for those who are mentally ill, for those whose pasts are scarred by abuse. I imagine resources to help people get past the mistakes they've made.

How can Patchwork even begin to bring justice to these situations? We don't provide financial assistance or jobs or counseling or housing or health care.

But we are a witness to the injustice. I believe that is no small thing.

We are also a place of acceptance and support. We are a place where people come together to try to learn from and understand each other. We are a place that runs on faith that there is a better way.

We are not alone. We are part of a much larger community of congregations and organizations and individuals who are working together to fight injustice. I believe that Patchwork embodies the words of Isaiah 58, and as part of a community working to remove the yoke of oppression, we can become the restorer of streets to live in.

Patchwork's Neighborhood Hospitality can be difficult to describe to someone who has never experienced it themselves—someone who has never walked into our building on a Monday morning to see a group of people clustered around the kitchen table talking, drinking coffee, eating donuts, and charging their cell phones. We're not a day shelter. We're not a soup kitchen. We have a food pantry, but we don't provide any additional financial aid.

We are . . . something else.

Each day is varied. It has moments that are enjoyable as our guests joke with us, and we are able to provide exactly what they need. But there are also moments that are difficult when we meet people whose needs are great, whose resources are limited, and for whom we have no good answers.

Stories have always been part of Patchwork. It is the individual stories from life at Patchwork that show what Patchwork is and why we're so different. They, more than any statistic, truly illustrate our impact and what justice looks like here. What follows is one story, the parable of the rake.

John and I live a few blocks from Patchwork Central near downtown Evansville. During apple season, I was raking up apples in front of my house when a big, burly guy with a cigarette dangling from his lips stopped on the sidewalk next to me and said, "Lemme see your rake," in a tone that suggested he simply wanted to examine my rake more closely.

Confused, I handed it to him.

He turned and, without a word, continued walking down the sidewalk. I yelled after him, but he didn't respond.

Who steals a rake?

The rake seemed to be gone for good, but several hours later, he showed up at our front door to return it. He said thanks, and when John asked if he'd gotten good use out of the rake, he said he had.

It was incredibly bizarre in so many ways.

Like a proper parable, there are many readings of the story. In one, it is a story of hospitality and community. This is what we do at Patchwork. Someone, anyone, walks through the doors at Patchwork and asks for something. More often than not, we try to provide it for him or her if we can.

It's an automatic reaction to someone in need, as illustrated by my story of the rake.

Standing in front of my house amid the rotting apples, there was a slow-motion moment when I watched my arm automatically extend to offer the guy my rake while my brain overthought it: "My rake? Why would you want my rake? Why shouldn't I give you my rake? What would this guy do with it? He's still waiting for a response. Is he joking? Hey, arm, what are you doing? I'm not sure that is a good idea . . ."

At Patchwork, we offer resources to people in a similar way. We extend a number of things:

- Showers for guests who can't or choose not to shower at the homeless shelters
- A cup of coffee, complete with a few packets of sugar that we've searched the entire kitchen to find
- A food order from the food pantry for the family of nine whose head of household comes in right before we close and without the correct paperwork
- A cake for the children's program's biggest bully when she pounds on the door that's locked because it's Friday and the building is officially closed
- Green tomatoes to the nameless people who excitedly pick them from our garden because you can't buy them in the store (but look! Patchwork actually grows green tomato plants!)
- Respect and conversation for someone angry and frustrated
- A piece of art that a child created in our children's program to take home so she can give her mother something beautiful
- Joy and safety for a child in a circle of other children and adults listening to a story about the sunshine and rain and getting sprayed with water from a squirt bottle

- A parent at our back-to-school sale who can get some school supplies for her family (even belts for their uniforms and flash drives!) without having to prove her low income or drag her children out of bed to prove they exist

Of course, by offering, we open ourselves up to an element of risk—as in the parable of the rake. Giving to others is a risk. Once you give something, you lose control over that thing and how the recipient uses it or even how the recipient receives it. You may feel your gift is misused. Or stolen. Or not properly appreciated. The gift could inadvertently make a bad situation worse. Or only offer a surface solution that doesn't address the larger societal forces that created the need.

Or it could be just what someone needed. It could return in the end with value added, like a great story to tell.

There is a risk in what we do at Patchwork, but this risk is inherent in our mission. In risking, we draw together and create interdependencies. We learn. We—as Patchwork's official tagline reminds us—create community.

And it is not only about us, the ones typically cast in the giving or serving role. Our guests and visitors feel that this is their community too, one that they contribute to and help to create. There is much that they are able to give back in return, and we receive it.

Today, Larry, a neighbor, sits at a table wearing a T-shirt emblazoned with an almost life-size portrait of Mr. Rogers and the words "It's All Good . . . in the Hood" printed boldly across the top and bottom. He comes in regularly for a cup of coffee and occasionally for food from our food pantry. Last summer, he decided I was dressed like a teacher. Ever since, he's asked me how the field trip is going. He asks again today. I laugh and go on my way. Yes, things are good in the hood. The coffee is hot and plentiful at Patchwork, and friends are gathered.

Larry is sitting and drinking coffee with Mary, a retired nurse who volunteers in Patchwork's Sozo Health Ministry. Like John, who created the Sozo Health Ministry in 2015, she spends a lot of time checking blood pressure, listening to people describe their symptoms, and dropping everything to drive someone to an appointment they're about to miss or even to the ER if she finds a need. She also wipes down tables, organizes donated items, and advises people on their life choices in a way only she can get away with. When she leaves at the end of every morning, she apologizes for not having done much. She does not speak the truth.

Cheryl sits with Larry and Mary. Last week Cheryl made bologna sandwiches for everyone. It began with her polling everyone at Patchwork: "Is anybody going to Simpson's Supermarket? I want to get some lunch meat. I think the people here would like some lunch meat."

She was thinking of her fellow morning guests. Recently we had not had many of our usual pastries and breakfast treats from the food bank for our guests to eat with their coffee. She wanted to help contribute to the good of the group. Eventually she found two food pantry clients who were headed toward the supermarket. They agreed to give her a ride, and she returned later with her lunch meat and distributed it to other Patchwork visitors. A volunteer made her a couple of sandwiches to take home.

Cheryl is one of our regulars. She lives nearby and stops in on most mornings for a cup of coffee and some conversation. She's on disability, doesn't own a car, and enjoys having Patchwork as part of her daily routine. Earlier, she told Shawn, one of our office staff, "I'm so glad I found Patchwork. I've met friends here. I can get bread when I need bread. I put it in my refrigerator so it stays fresh and eat it."

Eugene walks into the main office and sits down to talk to Shawn. He has a mental illness that led to violent incidents and an arrest. Now some neighbors help him manage his medication, and things are better. He is still banned from many other neighborhood institutions, but he's welcome at Patchwork. He starts to tell Shawn about his concerns about the Antichrist, but Shawn stops him. "It's Monday morning. If we're going to talk, it has to be about something positive, OK?"

"How 'bout them Colts?" he responds.

There is a flow of foot traffic through our main office. Men and women check in to take showers. Families wait patiently while Shawn checks with a call center to find out if they are eligible for food. Al and his therapy parrot, Midler, stop in to talk. Someone needs to use the phone. Someone else is trying to find which agencies help with bus tokens or gas to get to work.

Each person contributes to this thing that is Patchwork Central, constructing the space that we all share together. Each of these individuals owns and shapes the direction of Patchwork at least as much as I do in my role as an administrator here, and this is how it has always been.

Each day that the building is open, people enter and exchange gifts. It requires trust and it is risky, but Patchwork is built from those gifts and the community they create.

Patchwork Central: http://patchwork.org/

AMY RICH is the co–executive director of Patchwork Central, located in Evansville, Indiana. She is an artist, writer, gardener, and resident of one of the neighborhoods that Patchwork serves.

9

FRIENDS AND NEIGHBORS

Photographs from the Open Door Community

Calvin Kimbrough

Created in the image of God,
we are created in the image of God.
Human beings all over God's earth,
created in the image of God.

As a photographer, I make images with cameras, lenses, film, light, my eye, my vision, another's visage, and their eyes. This work, inspired by God's spirit, sometimes opens a door into the soul, revealing God's image.

I began making portrait photographs at the Open Door Community in 1992. From 2004 until 2016, I lived, worked, sang, played, and prayed at 910 Ponce de Leon Avenue in Atlanta. These images of our friends from the streets come from that home. They flow from the works of mercy and justice—the work of our household. Created in the image of God, these men and women open doors into God's soul. All are deserving of housing, food, health care, and a living wage. What is so difficult about sharing God's given abundance for the building of the beloved community among us?

Open Door Community Atlanta: https://opendoor community.org/

As a pastor, filmmaker, photographer, mentor, teacher, and song leader, **CALVIN KIMBROUGH** has been providing leadership on the margins for a just society for more than forty years. He completed BS and MA degrees at Tennessee Technological University in 1969 and 1971. He completed his master of divinity degree at Candler School of Theology at Emory University in 1975. In 1977, he helped found the Patchwork Central Community in Evansville, Indiana, living and working in an inner-city neighborhood there for twenty-seven years. From 2004 until 2016, he lived and worked at the Open Door Community, a residential community in the Catholic Worker tradition. He has been honored as one of 175 Makers of History at Emory University, a distinguished alumnus of Candler School of Theology and of Tennessee Tech.

10

ADVOCATING FOR CHILDREN

Trisha Brown, Yvonne Mans, and Sally Carr

THE INDIANA CHILD ADVOCATES NETWORK is made up of local programs that recruit, train, and supervise community volunteers for the tough but rewarding job of helping children through the court process and on to better lives in their own homes with a relative or an adoptive family. Once trained, a volunteer (court-appointed special advocate, or CASA; in some communities called GAL, *guardian ad litem*) is appointed by the judge to advocate for an abused or neglected child by providing objective information and recommendations.

Three of the Vanderburgh County CASA volunteer coordinators responded to the following questions: (1) How would you describe the work you do at CASA? (2) How/why were you attracted to this work? (3) Working with young people in difficult circumstances can be both challenging and rewarding. Would you be willing to share one of your greatest challenges or rewards since you have been with CASA? Here are their responses.

Trisha Brown

I was a family case manager (FCM) with the Division of Child Services (DCS) for over fifteen years and saw how much children needed the intervention of a court-appointed special advocate (CASA). I have been with CASA now for eleven years, and it amazes me what CASA volunteers are able to do with children and what services CASA volunteers can get in place for those same kids.

When working with DCS, I saw so many ways that family case managers, for reasons of policy or protocol, were unable to help children directly.

Here is just one example of the ways a CASA might positively affect the outcome of a case. A four-year-old girl had spent three years with a foster family. Her mother suffered from mental illness but was not willing to seek mental health care or take prescribed medications, so the child was removed from the home. Unfortunately, when the child's case came to court, sufficient evidence was not presented, and she was reunited with her birth mother. The biological mother soon began to take meth, a new court case was opened, and a CASA was assigned to the case. That case dragged on for three and a half years, at the end of which the mother's rights were terminated. Throughout this ordeal, the child continued to recognize her foster parents as her true family. In the end, happily, the child was adopted by the foster parents; the CASA was vital in this process.

Yvonne Mans

Wow, how complicated is the work at CASA! In the first place, it is exhausting. But that is certainly not the part that keeps me coming back every day. It is both challenging and extremely rewarding. I think what I like most is working with my volunteers. They are the most dedicated people on earth. I love being here for them to help them navigate the confusing maze that is the child welfare system. I love answering questions and watching them answer the challenge to grow into ever more effective advocates for children in so many ways.

How was I attracted to this work? I saw an old, rickety CASA billboard standing above a street in Evansville, Indiana, in the nineties. I passed it many times until the trees grew around and partially obscured it, and I always thought, *Hmm, that sounds like something I'd like to try.* I was a stay-at-home mom then and couldn't find the time. But my boys grew up, and I went back to school for my third degree, my master's in social work. Since I had been thinking about CASA, I thought it would be the perfect time to try it and a good way to get back in the social work field. So I interviewed and trained to become a volunteer. I thought I wanted to be a family therapist. But once I began advocating for children as a CASA, there was no turning back.

This work is a calling. It is difficult. Heart-wrenching. Frustrating. Sometimes maddening. It is not for the fainthearted. Sometimes it's devastating. It takes determination, persistence, and a spirit that never gives up. But the amazing thing is that even if you don't possess these attributes naturally, if this is your calling, your passion, you will find those strengths and abilities within yourself, pull them out, and both challenge and nurture yourself to master them because you know these kids have no one else but you. That is perhaps not what attracted me to this work, but it keeps me here. I see that process not only in myself but also in the volunteers I "coordinate." It is awesome to see the best come out in people to accomplish life-changing safety, permanency, and stability for children through the child welfare and court process—and sometimes in spite of it.

This is my reward for this work: when I watch CASA volunteers do the hard work of gathering all the facts from everyone involved in a child's case, read about their visits with the children, and listen to their stories about the children; when CASA volunteers answer the challenge to do more than they are comfortable doing, perhaps attempting to reason with parents who are less than pleasant to be around, perhaps speaking up in court, perhaps making that same phone call over and over and over again to get someone to respond and answer their questions, perhaps overcome the fear of dealing with professionals they feel intimidated by; when I see CASA volunteers grow through these things, put it all together, go against all other forces and win for children, that's my reward. One CASA volunteer, who has more years of experience than most told me, after a court hearing where she had put it all together, prepared her argument, spoke out in court, and gotten the ruling she knew the children needed, "That is the first time I felt like I made a difference." And she did. That was the reward that makes all the rest worth it.

Sally Carr

My job is to coordinate the CASA volunteers' work with the parents, children, DCS workers, courts, and service providers and to keep records of court procedures, dates, and other information pertinent to each case. I must be informed about current laws and familiar with DCS rules and changes relative to CHINS (child in need of services) and termination cases CASA is appointed to. I help make sure all releases are secured and signed, which allows the volunteers access to protected information. I support the volunteers and help them in their work.

I had been a volunteer for seven years before starting to work in the CASA office. When my own children were growing up, we often had their friends—who may have had difficulties at home—stay with us. At one point, I had a sixteen-year-old foster teenager move in, and I became his mother. I strongly believe that each child should have the opportunity to become the best that they can become. Oftentimes, it takes some encouragement from someone on their side.

I prefer to work with older children; sometimes, this is the last chance to change their lives in a positive way. I have been blessed in that many of the teens I have worked with have stayed in touch after they left the child welfare system. Some have graduated from college, others have married, and some struggle—sadly—with the same addictions their parents had. My heart goes out to these young adults, as I feel we failed them. Everyone needs to know that someone is on their side.

Indiana Child Advocates Network: http://www.child advocatesnetwork.org/

TRISHA BROWN has a bachelor of social work from the University of Southern Indiana. She worked with the Division of Child Services for seventeen years and has been with Evansville (Indiana) CASA for eleven.

YVONNE MANS was a CASA volunteer at Vanderburgh County CASA for six years. During that time, she joined the staff as a volunteer coordinator. She has worked with CASA volunteers for thirteen years. She holds an associate's degree in early childhood education and bachelor's and master's degrees in social work and is a licensed social worker.

With an accounting background, **SALLY CARR** managed several offices; while managing a local radio station in 1995, she became a CASA volunteer. With a strong passion for the needs of these children and their families, she took a position on the CASA staff in 2001, which has been the most rewarding work she has ever done. She is looking at achieving twenty-five years of service to CASA next year.

11

BOOKS TO OPEN
YOUNG MINDS

For Preschool through Middle School

Kamela Jordan

READING IS ONE OF THE best ways to open the mind. Books are a window into another world, a door into another culture, a glimpse into someone else's life. Stories tug at the heartstrings and kindle compassion for their heroes. They inform us about unfamiliar places and ways of life. They plant the seeds of understanding, and as understanding grows, fear and hate and condemnation wither away.

Picture books and chapter books, true stories and fiction and poetry, stories of immigrants and refugees, kids with disabilities and kids with two moms and kids in poverty—open a cover and step into another world!

An Introduction to Differences

Gila Monsters Meet You at the Airport, by Marjorie Weinman Sharmat. A boy from New York City moves to Arizona and has to overcome his fear of "different."

Different Just Like Me, by Lori Mitchell. April goes on errands with her mom and sees all kinds of different people, but she notices that just like her, they like to draw, push elevator buttons, and eat turkey sandwiches.

If You Don't Read Anything Else, Try . . .

Anything illustrated by E. B. Lewis. African American artist E. B. Lewis illustrates stories of Ethiopian folktales, African American pioneers, and regular kids, bringing such beauty to ordinary people that you want to meet them all. Some favorites include *A Circle Unbroken*, *Across the Alley*, *Fire on the Mountain*, *My Best Friend*, and *Talkin' about Bessie*.

Africa

The Color of Home, by Mary Hoffman. A picture book tells the moving story of Hassan, a Somali first grader who was forced to flee his war-torn homeland and make a new home in America.

A Gift for Sadia, by Marie Fritz Perry. The friendship of a wounded Canada goose helps a young Somali girl accept her new life in America.

Brothers in Hope, by Mary Williams. This Caldecott Honor Book tells the story of the arduous journey made by the Lost Boys of Sudan. Eight-year-old Garang, orphaned by a civil war, must find the strength to lead other boys as they trek hundreds of miles to safety.

Home of the Brave, by Katherine Applegate. This is the beautiful free-verse story of a young Sudanese refugee boy newly arrived in the United States.

The Red Pencil, by Andrea Davis Pinkney. Amira's life is shattered when her village in Sudan is destroyed by war. But in the refugee camp, she begins to find hope and new possibilities through the gift of a single red pencil.

Mufaro's Beautiful Daughters, by John Steptoe. This Caldecott Honor Book tells a Cinderella story from Zimbabwe.

African American

Henry's Freedom Box: A True Story from the Underground Railroad, by Ellen Levine, illustrated by Kadir Nelson. An award-winning author and illustrator team up to tell this stirring story of a slave who mails himself to freedom.

Aunt Harriet's Underground Railroad in the Sky, by Faith Ringgold. Cassie takes flight on an imaginary journey following the underground railway.

I, Too, Am America, by Langston Hughes. Langston Hughes's classic poem, paired with beautiful illustrations, tells the story of African American Pullman porters who collect books, magazines, and albums left behind by passengers and then toss them into the wind to spread knowledge and culture to everyone in the world.

I Have a Dream, by Martin Luther King Jr., illustrated by Kadir Nelson. Introduce kids to one of the most famous speeches in history and follow along with an audio recording of Dr. King himself.

Brown Girl Dreaming, by Jacqueline Woodson. This Newbery Honor Book and National Book Award winner features the author's vivid poems of growing up African American in the 1960s and 1970s.

This Is the Rope: A Story from the Great Migration, by Jacqueline Woodson. In this beautifully illustrated book, a rope passed down through the generations frames an African American family's story as they journey north during the time of the Great Migration.

The Crossover, by Kwame Alexander. This 2015 Newbery Medal winner is a novel in verse about fourteen-year-old twin basketball stars Josh and Jordan: a story of sports, family, and racial identity.

One Crazy Summer, by Rita Williams-Garcia. In this Newbery Honor Book and National Book Award finalist, Delphine and her two younger sisters travel to California to stay with the mother they barely know. It is the summer of 1968, and their mother, who resents their intrusion, wants them to attend the Black Panther summer camp.

Asia

Half Spoon of Rice: A Survival Story of the Cambodian Genocide, by Icy Smith. Nine-year-old Nat and his family are driven from their home, separated from each other, and, after many days of marching through jungle and countryside, are forced to work in the rice fields, where Nat concentrates on survival.

Running Shoes, by Frederick Lipp. With the help of a pair of running shoes, Sophy, a determined young girl living in an impoverished Cambodian village, fulfills her dream of going to school.

Little Cricket, by Jacquelyn M. Brown. When the Vietnam War throws their lives into turmoil, twelve-year-old Kia and her Hmong family must flee the mountains of Laos to a refugee camp in Thailand and eventually to the alien world of Saint Paul, Minnesota.

Inside Out and Back Again, by Thanhha Lai. This series of poems chronicles the journey of a young girl, her mother, and her brothers as they leave Vietnam and resettle in Alabama. It is a Newbery Honor Book and winner of the National Book Award.

The Lotus Seed, by Sherry Garland. A young Vietnamese girl saves a lotus seed and carries it with her everywhere to remind her of a brave emperor and the homeland she has to flee.

The Name Jar, by Yangsook Choi. Unhei is nervous that her new classmates won't be able to pronounce her Korean name, so she tells them that in a week, she will choose a new name from a jar. But while she practices becoming Suzy, Laura, and Amanda, someone discovers her real name and steals the jar.

A Piece of Home, by Jeri Watts. When Hee Jun moves from Korea to West Virginia, he suddenly becomes a "different" kid instead of just one of the crowd. Then the discovery of a familiar flower growing in a new friend's garden helps his family begin to put down roots and feel at home.

The Thing about Luck, by Cynthia Kadohata. Twelve-year-old Japanese American Summer must make her own luck out of bad luck when an emergency takes her parents back to Japan, leaving her to help her grandparents bring in the harvest. Generations and culture clash in this National Book Award finalist.

How My Parents Learned to Eat, by Ina Friedman. An American sailor courts a young Japanese woman, and each tries, in secret, to learn the other's way of eating.

The Balkans

My Childhood under Fire, by Nadja Halilbegovich. Nadja is just a normal twelve-year-old in Sarajevo until one day, school is suddenly canceled and gunfire and mortar shells drive her family and neighbors to hide in the basement.

Gleam and Glow, by Eve Bunting. After his home is destroyed by war, eight-year-old Viktor finds hope in two goldfish that have survived and multiplied in the garden pond. This book is beautifully illustrated with oil paintings.

Hispanic

The House on Mango Street, by Sandra Cisneros. This critically acclaimed coming-of-age classic is the poignant story of Esperanza Cordero, a young Latina girl growing up in Chicago. Taught in both grade schools and universities, the book has been translated all over the world.

Don't Say a Word, Mama / No Digas Nada, Mamá, by Joe Hayes. Rosa and Blanca are so generous and such good gardeners. What is Mama to do when she winds up with more corn, tomatoes, and red-hot chilies than she can eat? This is a bilingual tale.

Under the Mambo Moon, by Julia Durango. At Marisol's father's music store, customers from around Latin America come looking for songs to remind them of home. Durango's poems sizzle with the rhythms of merengue, vallenatos, salsa, and samba.

Lupita Mañana, by Patricia Beatty. After her father dies in a fishing boat accident, thirteen-year-old Lupita must help her family survive. Along with her brother Salvador, she sneaks across the border from Mexico to the United States in hopes of finding work that will make a better *mañana* (tomorrow) for her family back home.

Middle East

The White Zone, by Carolyn Marsden. As American bombs fall on Baghdad during the Iraq War, ten-year-old cousins Nouri and Talib witness the growing violence between Sunni and Shiite Muslims.

Four Feet, Two Sandals, by Karen Lynn Williams and Khadra Mohammed. Two Afghan girls in a refugee camp in Pakistan each find one sandal from a matching pair. Deciding that it is better to share the sandals than for each to wear only one, they soon become friends.

One Green Apple, by Eve Bunting. While on a school field trip to an orchard to make cider, a young immigrant named Farah gains self-confidence when the green apple she picks perfectly complements the other students' red apples.

The Sandwich Swap, by Queen Rania Al Abdullah and Kelly Di-Pucchio. Who doesn't want to read a book written by a real queen? Lily and Salma are best friends, but will peanut butter and hummus sandwiches pull them apart?

Shooting Kabul, by N. H. Senzai. Escaping from Taliban-controlled Afghanistan in the summer of 2001, eleven-year-old Fadi and his family immigrate to the San Francisco Bay Area, where Fadi schemes to return to the Pakistani refugee camp where his little sister was accidentally left behind.

The Breadwinner, by Deborah Ellis. Because the Taliban rulers of Kabul, Afghanistan, impose strict limitations on women's freedom and behavior, eleven-year-old Parvana must disguise herself as a boy so that she can work to help her family survive after her father's arrest.

The Green Bicycle, by Haifaa Al-Mansour. Since girls do not ride bikes in Riyadh, Saudi Arabia, eleven-year-old Wadjda has to scheme to get her own.

Native American

The Birchbark House, by Louise Erdrich. Omakayas, a seven-year-old Native American girl of the Ojibwa tribe, lives through the joys of summer and the perils of winter on an island in Lake Superior in 1847. The first in a series of wonderful novels for middle grades.

Children of the Longhouse, by Joseph Bruchac. When Ohkwa'ri overhears a group of older boys planning a raid on a neighboring village, he reports them to his Mohawk elders. He knows he has done the right thing, but now the older boys are plotting to hurt him during the village lacrosse game. Will Ohkwa'ri be able to follow the path of peace?

Thunder Boy Jr., by Sherman Alexie, illustrated by Yuyi Morales. Thunder Boy Jr. is named after his dad, but he wants a name all his own. This is a charming book from a National Book Award–winning author and Caldecott Honor–winning illustrator.

Between Earth & Sky: Legends of Native American Sacred Places, by Joseph Bruchac. This book offers prose poetry and luminous paintings of ancient lands and traditions.

Gender and Sexuality

Tatterhood and Other Tales, edited by Ethel Johnston Phelps. A collection of twenty-five traditional tales from around the world features spirited heroines with extraordinary courage and wit.

Nate Ballerino, by Kimberly Brubaker Bradley. After seeing a ballet performance, Nate decides he wants to learn to dance, but his brother Ben tells him that only girls can be ballerinas.

In Our Mother's House, by Patricia Polacco. Marmee and Meema raise their African American daughter, Asian American son, and Caucasian daughter in a lively, close-knit neighborhood.

And Tango Makes Three, by Justin Richardson. This award-winning book tells the true story of two inseparable male penguins at the Central Park Zoo who hatch a motherless egg.

My Two Uncles, by Judith Vigna. Elly's grandfather doesn't want Uncle Ned to bring Phil to his birthday party in this story of rejection, growth, and family.

Mini Mia and Her Darling Uncle, by Pija Lindenbaum. Ella loves her eccentric uncle Tommy, but when his new boyfriend, Fergus, starts joining their special outings, trouble is not far away.

Be Who You Are, by Jennifer Carr. Nick was born in a boy's body but has always felt like a girl inside. Nick's supportive family says, "Always remember to be who you are, Nick." With their support, Nick decides to be addressed as *she* and to be named Hope. This book is based on the author's experiences with her children.

Disability

Out of My Mind, by Sharon Draper. Fifth-grade Melody is smarter than everyone in her class, maybe even smarter than the teacher. But cerebral palsy prevents her from speaking, and everyone thinks she's mentally challenged. Finally, new technology gives her brilliance a voice. With thousands of five-star reviews on Amazon, this book is a powerful reminder that people with disabilities are fully human.

My Buddy, by Audrey Osofsky. A golden retriever helps a young boy with muscular dystrophy dress, go to school, and play.

Thank You, Mr. Falker, by Patricia Polacco. In the author's true story of growing up dyslexic, learning to read makes her feel stupid until her new fifth-grade teacher steps in.

Susan Laughs, by Jeanne Willis. Susan laughs, sings, rides, and swings. She gets angry, she gets sad, she is good, and she is bad. Not until the last adorable picture do readers see that Susan uses a wheelchair.

Looking After Louis, by Lesley Ely. Louis has autism, but through a special game of soccer, his classmates find a way to join him in his world. Then they can include Louis in theirs.

My Friend Isabelle, by Eliza Woloson. Isabelle and Charlie are friends. They both like to draw, dance, read, and play at the park. They both like to eat Cheerios. They both cry if their feelings are hurt. And, like most friends, they are also different from each other. Isabelle has Down syndrome. Charlie doesn't.

All Dogs Have ADHD and *All Cats Have Asperger Syndrome,* by Kathy Hoopmann. These two titles offer a playful introduction to two of the common learning disabilities children see in their classrooms.

Religion

Magid Fasts for Ramadan, by Mary Matthews, illustrated by E. B. Lewis. In this beautifully illustrated introduction to the beliefs and practices of Islam, Mama and Baba tell Magid he isn't old enough to fast, but he doesn't want to wait.

The Garden of My Imaan, by F. Zia. Aliya is embarrassed to practice her Muslim faith at school, but the arrival of Marwa, a fellow sixth grader who's a strict Muslim, helps Aliya find the courage to be true to her beliefs.

Hanukkah, Shmanukkah, by Esme Codell. In this Jewish spin on *A Christmas Carol*, Old Scroogemacher is visited on the last night of Hanukkah by three rabbis who take him on a journey from the time of the Maccabees to present day.

Passover Story: The Boy Who Helped Moses, by Rachel Mintz. Eli, the youngest son in a Hebrew slave family, becomes an assistant to Moses as he leads the Israelite people out of Egypt.

Buddha Stories, by Demi. This is a collection of ten Jataka tales from Buddha.

The Broken Tusk, by Uma Krishnaswami. This is a collection of stories about the pantheon of Hindu gods, centering on the sometimes greedy, sometimes impulsive, but always generous elephant-headed Ganesha.

The Hiding Place (Young Readers Edition), by Corrie ten Boom. A Dutch Christian family's faith compels them to risk their lives to rescue Jews from the Nazis. Eventually they are arrested and sent to a concentration camp, but even when they are surrounded by death and despair, faith gives them courage and hope.

Poverty

The Orange Shoes, by Trinka Hakes Noble. Delly Porter enjoys the feel of soft dirt beneath her feet, but when her classmates make her feel ashamed of having no shoes, she must learn to find value in the things money cannot buy.

The Kite, by Luis Garay. After his father's death, Francisco must help his mother make ends meet by selling newspapers in the marketplace, especially with a new baby on the way. Will he ever be able to buy the beautiful kite he longs for to soar above his squalid city?

Last Stop on Market Street, by Matt de la Peña. In this Newbery Medal and Caldecott Honor winner, CJ wants to know why he and his grandma always ride the bus while others take their own cars. Why doesn't he have an iPod like other boys? CJ's grandmother helps him see the beauty and fun in their own lives.

Diversity Council: https://www.diversitycouncil.org/

A graduate of Taylor University in Indiana, **KAMELA JORDAN** worked as office and communications coordinator at Diversity Council in Rochester, Minnesota, until 2018.

12

THE SWEET SPOT OF CLIMATE ACTION

Jim Poyser

My Journey Away from Hopelessness

About a decade ago, I had a can't-fall-back-to-sleep awakening about our climate crisis. Prior to 2007, I would read newspaper articles about climate change or occasionally see a documentary, but the message of urgency just didn't quite sink in.

However, I distinctly remember the day in 2007 when I read a story about the North Pole becoming circumnavigable—years ahead of scientific projections, meaning, of course, that the Arctic was melting much more quickly than had been predicted.

Something about that story hit me in a way from which I have never quite recovered. It is still a mystery to me why *this* moment and *this* story, but it's partly due to the amount of attention I was paying coupled with the vulnerability I was feeling that day.

Simply put, I broke down and cried uncontrollably for a world in an unstoppable downward spiral.

There are times I'd like to go back to an ostensibly simpler time, when I wasn't so obsessed with planetary-wide climate change, but I haven't had any success. Can't put that proverbial genie back in the blissful-ignorance bottle.

Part of the problem, I'm sure, is the persistent resistance to accepting the consensus science about climate change. From everyday people to the upper echelons of our US government, people refuse to reckon with the impact humans are having on the environment.

I guess they think that pollution just goes on up into space, where it is lost to the cosmos.

Then there are the prickly peccadilloes of normal life: the leaf blowers, the plastic straws, the idling cars . . . the everyday damage we do with our consumption behaviors.

Take straws, for example. Some years ago, I was in a restaurant. As I peered across the room, all I saw was a crop of straws sticking up out of every glass. Some customers had multiple glasses and thus multiple straws. Suddenly a visual pun erupted in my mind: a straw bale made entirely of straws.

I laughed aloud, but couldn't forget the image, and so in 2015, I set about making that image manifest. Support came from the DaVinci Pursuit in Indianapolis, and I partnered with a similarly straw-hating restaurateur, Neal Brown, to collect his used straws to build my straw bale.

The straw bale was ugly. For a while, I was glad that it was, since the problem of straws and plastic waste *is* a decidedly unattractive externality of human consumption. But there are limits to even what I can stand. I decided to make another, more appealing straw bale, this time collecting thousands of straws from numerous Indianapolis restaurants in a variety of colors: pink, black, clear, green.

Contemplating the ugly straw bale

Now I have an attractive straw bale to put on display; well, at least I can stand the sight of it. And I take it to schools and work with kids on conservation practices; with me, these students reach out to local restaurants to encourage them to stop handing out straws automatically to customers.

My ask is simply that restaurants give you a straw only if you ask for one. Stop automatically providing straws!

About ten restaurants have signed a resolution stating just that, but on my subsequent visits to these restaurants, there are still forests of straws. Old habits are hard to break—even if they are largely unnecessary and ultimately destructive habits.

Magical Convergence

But environmental conditions continued to deteriorate, and despite a worldwide recession, carbon emissions continued to rise. I felt helpless in the face of such enormity.

And the Arctic continued to melt.

While the planet heated up, so did I—in anger. I became more intolerant—of car idlers, meat grillers, leaf blower-ers, high noon lawn mower-ers, extravagant farters—of everyone, really, even including myself, as a kind of automatic self-loathing kicked in.

It appeared that here in the United States, at least, we were on an unconscious trajectory to ruin our little nest. Maybe some collective death wish was in play. Or perhaps the human infestation was simply out of control.

There's no question who will suffer the most from this human pollution: communities of color and those of low socio-economic status. We also know the elderly and the very young are subject to the worst of our externalities as well.

I lucked into something in 2012 that proved to be the fulcrum I needed. *An Inconvenient Truth* was released in 2007 and then morphed into a slideshow presentation one could be trained on to then present to others. I missed the email invite, but my wife did not, who fortunately shared it with me, imagining how good I would be in that role.

So I took the training, and at the tender age of fifty-four, I started to deliver the first ever PowerPoints of my life. Turns out I was horrible at it, but I persisted and got more comfortable, and soon I began to put my own comic spin on the presentations, including a one-man theatrical show I called "Saving the World thru Bumper Stickers" and a game show called "The Ain't Too Late Show."

I did my slideshows in churches, art galleries, and colleges—even my living room. Then one day, I accepted an invitation to do the presentation in an elementary school, against my better judgment. I mean, what was I going to say to a bunch of ten- and eleven-year-olds about climate change? I didn't want them running screaming from the room.

The Basic Greenhouse Gases / Greenhouse Effect 101 was what I decided to present, and very quickly I realized the kids were already keen on the basics of climate change and were in fact working on projects at their school, like vermicomposting, recycling, building aquaponics systems, designing a green roof, and planning for a beehive.

I walked out of that school feeling the kind of epiphany I had only read about in books and observed in movies. Suddenly, I knew what I wanted to do with the rest of life: work with kids on climate solutions.

This was in April 2013; by September 1, I had quit my newspaper job and was running a statewide nonprofit, Earth Charter Indiana, that was dedicated to addressing the climate crisis through education and the empowerment of youth.

Just to give you a taste, here is the opening paragraph to the Earth Charter's preamble:

We stand at a critical moment in Earth's history, a time when humanity must choose its future. As the world becomes increasingly interdependent and fragile, the future at once holds great peril and great promise. To move forward we must recognize that in the midst of a magnificent diversity of cultures and life forms we are one human family and one Earth community with a common destiny. We must join together to bring forth a sustainable global society founded on respect for nature, universal human rights, economic justice, and a culture of peace. Towards this end, it is imperative that we, the peoples of Earth, declare our responsibility to one another, to the greater community of life, and to future generations.

I still, six years later, shake my head in disbelief that it all came together in the way that it did. To call it luck would ignore the sweat equity of having spent all those hours trying to find a way to address the climate crisis. To call it the result of all this hard work would ignore the magic of luck and how when you ask from your heart for something to happen . . . it sometimes does.

But it also took two key friends to agree to donate the equivalent of about two-thirds of my existing annual income—this was enough comfort to make the leap, and then I was off and running.

Individual Stewardship Is Not Enough

Hallelujah! Now I could work on climate change full time, 'round the clock. My main audience in the beginning was kids. That's what my new Earth Charter Indiana job description was about: start a youth program to empower young people to address the climate crisis—now.

In the nineties, I was a schoolteacher, my wife was a schoolteacher (and now a principal), and my daughter was a schoolteacher (and now works with students on peace and justice and conflict resolution). In short, I had plenty of connections to teachers and schools.

At first, I'd go to a school and deliver a presentation on climate change. I'd count the number of kids, go home, add that number to a spreadsheet, and watch the number grow. I would proudly report those numbers to my board, to funders, and to prospective funders.

Pretty soon, I figured out I wasn't actually doing anything meaningful.

In fact, I was just one more adult standing up in front of these kids, yakking at them.

But once again, I got lucky. I started going to an Indianapolis public school called Sidener Academy. I got a meeting with the robotics club because they were wanting to do some kind of conservation project, and I suggested to them they might start with their lunch trays, which were made of polystyrene and were used and then discarded every day by the thousands.

They began to research polystyrene and subsequently produced a pretty impressive PowerPoint that IPS Superintendent Lewis Ferebee ended up hearing about. He invited these fifth graders into his office to discuss their project.

By now, a student at another school, IPS 84, had joined Sidener. Together, they presented their PowerPoint; Dr. Ferebee invited them to present to the entire school board. A month or so later, they did, and presto!—the school board announced they were moving away from polystyrene to recyclable cardboard.

I finally had a victory that meant something to me.

Since then, we've moved to a more ambitious project of zero-waste cafeterias, but as you can imagine, that will be a complicated project. But the journey is the destination, right? The point is that kids begin to think in systems, not isolated parts of a system that is probably broken anyway.

How can we reimagine what we are doing so we can reduce our harmful impact on the earth?

Turning to Cities

Earth Charter Indiana tried in 2013 and 2014 to convince the Environmental Rules Board of Indiana to get moving on a climate action plan for our state, but that effort failed. So I focused on working with kids in schools, recycling, and zero waste, along with gardens and beehives.

However, common sense dictates that individual behavioral changes are not enough: you have to change the system, create policy, and maybe even pass laws.

By 2016, having failed at this statewide level, we turned our attention to cities. Lots of other people had already figured this out, but we quickly realized that cities were where the action was when it came to climate change. We also quickly figured out that party affiliation wasn't an indicator of an elected official's interest in addressing climate change.

And this was where things got interesting—especially in the face of a new administration with outspoken denial of the overwhelming science of climate change. We started to get traction in cities run by Republicans.

Kids to the Rescue

The first city we got good feedback from will come as no surprise to those familiar with Mayor Jim Brainard's work in the city of Carmel. Brainard is a sustainability-focused mayor, known around the country for his beaucoup roundabouts and other fuel-saving, energy-efficient strategies.

ECI started working with a high school–aged student, Maddie Adkins, who took this idea of a municipal-based climate resolution directly to Mayor Brainard. With the support and assistance of Leslie Webb of Carmel Green Initiative, Adkins created a youth team called the Promise Project, and Carmel was off and running toward passing the state's first youth-led climate-recovery resolution. For all I know, it's the *only* all-Republican city (mayor and city council) in the country to adopt some kind of climate resolution.

Meanwhile, in Indianapolis, I was leading a group of young people in a similar process. Kids as young as twelve years old attended meetings with city engineers and city council members, talking about climate change and how Indianapolis could address it. We were fortunate to have a main champion, city-county council vice president Zach Adamson.

Adamson is well known to the environmental and social justice community in Indy. He's fought for many improvements to our community, and he took the climate-recovery resolution idea and ran with it, eventually finding a Republican co-sponsor for the bill.

These two resolution cities were neck and neck over the holidays in 2016–2017, before Carmel passed theirs first on February 20. One week later, Indianapolis passed its resolution, 20–4, the largest city in the country to pass a youth-led climate resolution.

By spring, a new mayor was in the mix, Steve Collier of Lawrence. Lawrence is a suburb of Indy, on the east side, and some of the students working on the Indianapolis resolution are actually residents of Lawrence. Mayor Collier had heard about students in his city educating others about climate change—and also doing something about it—and so he invited these Oaklandon Elementary students into his office to present on climate change and local action.

Summer interrupted the process a bit, but on September 5, these kids (fifth, sixth, and seventh graders) presented to their city council, who adopted the climate resolution unanimously.

So Lawrence is our third city to pass a resolution in response to youth efforts. It's important to note that two of the cities, Carmel and Lawrence, have Republican mayors, and in Indianapolis, the majority of Republicans on the city-county council voted for the resolution, ergo, the 20–4 margin.

At Earth Charter Indiana, we like that; in fact, we love that. There is nothing political about climate change; it's a scientific fact. The only way to solve it is to face it—together. Here in Indiana, it appears we are doing just that.

The Courage to Speak

Yes, a resolution is a mere promise, and these resolutions promise carbon neutrality by 2050 (Carmel's is open-ended with no due date), which is, according to the majority of climate scientists, not nearly fast enough to avert catastrophe.

Still, I believe it's a start. We can build momentum on climate change and send a signal to the country and beyond that in Indiana, party affiliation doesn't matter: together, we will take action to protect our children and grandchildren from climate change.

But as excited as I am about these cities, it's an Indiana city that has not yet officially passed a resolution that provides a memorable experience to share.

Columbus, Indiana, was in the mix early on, right there with Indy and Carmel. I'd been traveling to Columbus schools to try to get people interested in this resolution project, and in the process, I found an amazingly active school, St. Bartholomew.

Their teacher, Bridget Steele, is committed to reducing carbon footprint and being a good earth steward. She integrates this commitment into her regular curriculum and, in addition, formed a club to work on the climate-recovery resolution.

There is a group of local activists in Columbus called Energy Matters, who work on various efforts to inspire Columbus toward sustainability. Energy Matters, especially Barry Kastner, worked with Bridget and her kids to prepare to approach the city on this important issue.

St. B students interviewed their mayor, Jim Lienhoop, along with members of the city council. They worked with Energy Matters to devise a resolution that's different than the one used in Carmel, then Indy and Lawrence.

Finally, they got their chance to present to the city council on June 6, 2017.

I know the date precisely because it was my thirtieth wedding anniversary. But instead of dining with my wife in Indianapolis where we live, I traveled to Columbus to witness these eighth graders give their presentation.

There was a practice in the basement of city hall prior to the presentation. Bridget and Barry and their group—called the Climate Restoration Team—read from their script. There were about a half-dozen students, each with a paragraph or two.

Toward the end of the first run-through, a student named José took his turn. He paused, and that pause turned into an agonizing silence. Then he spoke, a syllable or two, nonsensical. Then he tried again—another pause, another burst of language. Slowly, he added more syllables, more words, but there was hesitation, consonants repeated, long pauses.

Clearly, José had a profound stuttering issue. What would have taken three or four minutes took much longer. I was concerned that the flow and impact of the presentation would be compromised, but even more, I was concerned for José and the embarrassment he might feel.

There was another run-through, and when it was time for José's turn, once again, it was a painful staccato performance. Bridget pulled him aside, and they went into another room to discuss.

They returned; José took another shot at it. No improvement.

But it was time to go upstairs to present to the city council.

Showtime. The St. B kids took turns reading from their prepared testimony, and toward the end came José.

Look. There's no Hollywood ending here. José did not suddenly find eloquence and blow everyone away with a soaring speech. Truth is, he had a very difficult time fighting through his stammer to deliver his paragraph. The city council and attendees were respectful and sat in silence as he struggled, and then he finally finished. The final two students read their paragraphs, and then they were done.

For me, I can't put Columbus in the success column, but I do put it in the courage column. Each of the kids had to face his or her fears to get up and speak to adults in power. But stop for a moment and think about José, not only intimidated by speaking to adults, but having to fight through a stuttering issue to do so.

At any point, José could have deferred to any of his fellow classmates to take on his paragraph. But he didn't. He wanted to speak, to have his voice heard as he advocated for his future.

I figure if José can get up there and face all these challenges, then we have no excuses not to do so as well.

I think about José whenever I start to descend into despair or judge others too harshly. Intolerance gets me nowhere; it's just a way to make others wrong so I can be right.

By focusing on youth, I have found the sweet spot of climate action. It just makes sense: We are handing a mess of a planet to our children. Why not give them the opportunity not only to participate in fixing it, but also to lead the effort in doing so?

Earth Charter: https://earthcharter.org/

JIM POYSER was born and raised in South Bend, Indiana, and attended Indiana University Bloomington, majoring in English and telecommunications. After stints as a housepainter, schoolteacher, journalist, and editor, he became executive director of Earth Charter Indiana. He lives on the White River in Indianapolis with his wife, Patricia Wildhack.